THE NUTS AND BOLTS OF
NURSING
LEADERSHIP

Your Toolkit for Success

ROSE O. SHERMAN

Inquiries about the book should be directed to: roseosherman@outlook.com

Author Website: www.emergingrnleader.com

ISBN: 978-1-7329127-1-7
Library of Congress Control Number: 2020925082

Published by Rose O. Sherman

Printed in the United States of America

ACKNOWLEDGMENTS

I have been privileged to teach nurse leaders like you for the past three decades. I continue to learn as much from you as you have from me. The stories that I present in this book are ones that you have shared with me. There has never been a more challenging time to be a nurse leader. Thank you for choosing a leadership role.

My colleagues at the American Organization of Nurse Executives, the American Organization of Perioperative Nurses, and the American Nurses Association have given me opportunities to share my leadership work on a national level. I am grateful for those experiences.

Nurse leaders stand on the shoulders of those who took time to mentor and guide them. I was fortunate to have many great nurse mentors, including the late Marie Basti, Dr. Anne Boykin, and Dr. Roxane Spitzer. I would not be where I am today without these three exceptional leaders. A special thank you to my colleague and friend, Dr. Joyce Batcheller. I could not ask for a better co-facilitator for our *Nuts and Bolts of Nursing Leadership* program.

To my family and new granddaughter, Beverly Rose, you have always been terrific in your support of my career and continually inspire me to do better work.

Introduction

Over the past two decades, I have taught nursing leadership to thousands of nurses, some new to their roles, others with decades of experience. There is so much to learn on one's leadership journey that it can be challenging to know where to begin. From radically different workforce demographics to emerging new technologies, the healthcare environment is experiencing rapid change. With these changes come new demands and expectations of nurse leaders. The recent crisis with COVID-19 has heightened our awareness of the vital need for nurse leaders to balance advocacy for staff with the organization's needs.

Moving from a clinical role to leadership requires a different mindset and new knowledge, skills, and competencies. Both nursing staff and leaders in healthcare organizations have high expectations of nurses who become leaders. Knowing what to do and what not to do in leadership today is essential. Nursing research demonstrates that frontline leaders are the linchpins in their organizations that drive recruitment, retention, and staff performance. Despite the challenges, nurses often take leadership roles without the tools they need to be successful.

First-time nurse leaders are usually amazed at the depth and scope of responsibilities in a leadership role. It can feel like being a novice nurse all over again. Taking a formal role in leading a unit, department, or clinical service is, in many ways, like running your own small business. Today, the average nurse manager in the United States has more than sixty direct staff reports and manages a multi-million-dollar budget. It is a complex role. Knowing where to focus your time and energy to meet all the expectations can be difficult, especially for new leaders.

The *Nuts and Bolts of Nursing Leadership* provides you with the essential knowledge, skills, and behaviors you need to become a successful leader, whether you are just beginning or have years of experience. In an easy-to-read format, each chapter includes stories of challenges that leaders have shared with me so that you can learn from their experiences. The book contains tactical advice and actionable strategies that you can apply to feel less overwhelmed and more confident. Let this book be your toolkit and practical guide to a successful leadership career, regardless of your clinical setting.

CONTENTS

Acknowledgments iii

Introduction. v

PART 1 TRANSITIONING INTO LEADERSHIP 1

1 Stepping into Leadership 3
2 Leading Yourself. 15
3 Building Trust and Authenticity. 27
4 Organizing Your Work. 37
5 Improving Your Decision-Making Skills 49
Part 1 References 59

PART 2 COMMUNICATING AND COLLABORATING
       IN LEADERSHIP ROLES 63

6 Mastering Communication 65
7 Giving Effective Feedback 79
8 Promoting Constructive Conflict. 91
9 Encouraging Diverse Thinking. 101
10 Developing a Coaching Mindset 109
Part 2 References 117

Part 3 Leading High- Performance Teams **121**

11 Building Cohesive Teams 123
12 Creating a Culture of Quality and Safety 135
13 Promoting Staff Engagement 145
14 Managing Resistance to Change 155
15 Fostering Individual and Team Resilience 163
Part 3 References 173

Part 4 Leading in Organizations **179**

16 Understanding Healthcare Reimbursement 181
17 Learning Budget Basics 193
18 Managing Your Staffing Resources 203
19 Developing a Strategic Mindset 215
20 Building Your Influence and Leadership Brand 225
Part 4 References 239

Part 5 Your Leadership Toolkit **245**

A 100 Day Nurse Leader Action Plan 247
A Staff Guide to Working with You 249
Go-To Questions for Difficult Conversations 251
Resiliency GROW Model Coaching Template 252
The Circle of Influence Tool 253
Questions to Ask Staff 254
To Build Your Brand - Know Who You Are as Leader 255
Read and Listen to Lead – Free Resources 256

About the Author 257

PART 1

TRANSITIONING INTO LEADERSHIP

"How we lead ourselves in life impacts
how we lead those around us."

MICHAEL HYATT

CHAPTER 1

STEPPING INTO LEADERSHIP

How did you decide to become a nurse leader? I frequently ask leaders this question. You quickly learn that each leader's journey is different. Some nurses choose to apply for leadership positions, but a surprising number will tell you that they "fell into leadership" and did not seek out the role. Often, nurses take their first position on an interim basis and discover that they have leadership talent. Others are encouraged by senior leaders or sometimes by their peers who see potential in them that they may not see in themselves.

Regardless of how you arrive, once you take that first leadership role, you quickly learn that being a nurse leader requires a different skill set than a clinical staff role. In many ways, it is like running a small business. Nurse managers today directly supervise more than sixty staff and are responsible for multi-million dollar budgets.[1] There are many new competencies to master which can feel like being a novice nurse all over again.[2] Even experienced leaders acknowledge challenges with managing their time and energy.

Every leadership role is different. When you move into a new leadership role, it is essential to understand the organizational expectations. Jessica did this when she accepted the nurse manager role in a busy critical-care unit. Although she had been a charge nurse in the same organization, she realized that her responsibilities were now different. Initially, Jessica was excited about the promotion, but then she became stressed. Her transition happened almost overnight. On Friday, she was a charge nurse where her shift responsibilities were clear. The following Monday, she received her new badge, a lab coat, and the keys to her office. She was assigned a nurse manager mentor but did not receive any formal leadership development before assuming the position. Jessica was not even sure how to organize her first week, so she called her mentor.

Jessica's mentor smiled, remembering a similar experience when she began in leadership. She urged Jessica to start by meeting with the director of critical care to review key expectations in her position description. Using her mentor's advice, Jessica formed a list of the following questions to ask her new boss:

- What are the essential priorities for my first 100 days?
- Is there a leadership competency model in this organization?
- What meetings should be on my calendar?
- Who are some key people with whom I should schedule an appointment?
- How frequently should we meet during the next three months?
- What key performance metrics should I monitor and discuss with you?
- How should I manage the questions that I have?
- What would a successful transition look like after the first three months?

YOUR FIRST 100 DAYS

Jessica's director answered all her questions. She told Jessica that the first 100 days in any new leadership role needed careful planning. She helped her to develop a 100-day transition plan (sample in Chapter 5). She also gave Jessica the following five tips to build trust and ensure success:

1. **MEET WITH ALL YOUR DIRECT REPORTS.**

   Whenever there is a change in leadership, the nursing staff will worry about how a new manager will affect them. A key success factor for the new nurse leader is to be proactive in alleviating this concern by scheduling a meeting with each staff member during the first 100 days. These meetings will provide you with an opportunity to build a relationship with each staff member, find out about their concerns, and seek support from them. Some questions to ask during these meetings include:

   - What are three things that you are proud of about this unit/department/organization?
   - What are the three things you would like to see change?
   - What do you most need me to do as your leader?
   - What are you most concerned that I might do?
   - What advice do you have for me?

2. **GAIN TRUST BY LISTENING AND OBSERVING.**

   To gain the staff's trust, you need to avoid rushing to judgment about *"what is wrong"* based on your observations. At the same time, you do need to take note of what you see. Listen during your conversations with staff and carefully observe what happens on the unit when you make rounds. During the first 100 days, new leaders should also reach out to stakeholders, including patients, interdisciplinary team members, and other department leaders. They will provide you with essential insights into your work setting, and you will want to build strong working relationships with them.

3. **Use your mentor as a sounding board.**

You want to build strong relationships with your staff but remember that they are not your leadership peers and should not be used as sounding boards when the topic is confidential. Instead, schedule time with your mentor to review your progress and discuss challenges.

4. **Expect some pushback.**

Some seasoned nurses will be threatened by having a younger nurse manager even if they have no interest in being a leader. Former peers and friends could become critical of your leadership. You can expect some staff to test your leadership. You might receive pushback on your decisions when you begin the position. It is important not to feel threatened when and if this occurs. Initially, you may not have the trust and respect of the whole group. Trust builds over time, and leaders need to earn it. Consider adopting a servant leader philosophy of leadership (discussed in Chapter 3). A servant leader looks to the staff's needs and asks themself how the staff can help them solve problems and promote personal development.

5. **Avoid Acting too quickly.**

Wise nurse leaders do not announce significant changes during their first 100 days and do not turn their departments upside down. Use this time to gather information and determine the next steps. Jessica may want to jump right in and make changes because she is knowledgeable about the unit. She should resist doing this until she assesses the impact of doing something new.

Five Exemplary Practices of Leadership

Meeting the expectations of nursing staff can seem daunting to new leaders. It is clear from the research that nurses leave leaders, not organizations. It is the frontline leader who is the linchpin for recruitment and retention.[3] Understanding what staff wants matters if your goal is to be the leader that no one wants to leave. An excellent leadership model to consider is Jim Kouzes and Barry Posner's evidence-based *The Five Practices of Exemplary Leadership® Model* (Figure 1).[4] Their work draws on more than 40 years of research and assessments done with five million leaders globally.

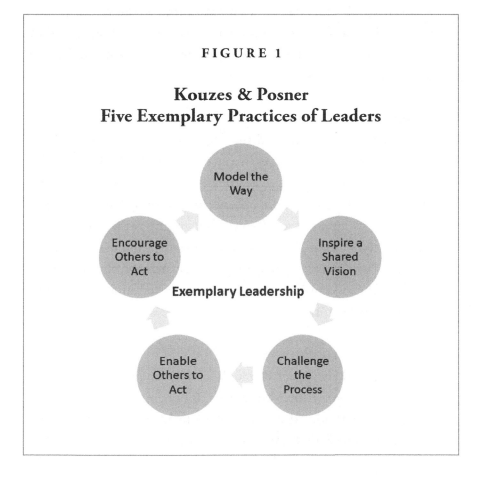

FIGURE 1

Kouzes & Posner
Five Exemplary Practices of Leaders

Based on their research, Kouzes and Posner identified the following five practices of exemplary leadership:

1. MODEL THE WAY

Model the way is a fundamental practice because it is how leaders earn, sustain, and build credibility. Influential leaders do what they say they will do. Before leaders can model the way, they need to clarify their values (discussed in Chapter 3). The leader's values need to be congruent with those of the organization. If your values conflict with your organization, it is not easy to effectively model the way. A second component to modeling the way is to "walk the talk." You set the example through your daily actions. It is difficult to counsel a staff member about tardiness if you are frequently late. When leading, your team watches you for the signals you send.

2. INSPIRE A SHARED VISION

The best leaders look toward the future with optimism and hope. They imagine the possibilities in any change and get others involved and inspired by asking, "what's next?" and "how can we contribute to this future direction?" They caution others about clinging to practices that are "sacred cows" but might not be right for the organization's future. When there is a new direction in the organization, they work hard to get everyone on board with the new vision. People want to know that what they do matters and will continue to matter in the future.

3. CHALLENGE THE PROCESS

Leaders should always actively look for ways to make things better, innovate, and grow their businesses. Challenge the status quo to bring new methods, ideas, and solutions into use. In healthcare, we talk about the importance of evidence-based practice, but these changes often come slowly. Even when there is promising research about a need to change practices, widespread adoption can take several decades. Leaders play a crucial role in establishing cultures to challenge old processes and implement change. Reward staff for innovation; otherwise, it will not become part of the culture. You must search for new opportunities and be willing to take risks. The best leaders learn to proceed until apprehended in approaching new challenges.

4. ENABLE OTHERS TO ACT

Success in any work requires a team effort. Leaders who enable others to act create a culture that fosters collaboration and builds trust. They make it possible for others to do their best work by maximizing their strengths versus focusing on their weaknesses. They willingly share power and develop others. Building a climate of trust on the team is an essential first step. Current research with younger staff indicates that leaders dedicated to developing others are much more successful in their recruitment and retention efforts. A vital job of any leader is to serve as a coach to help staff organize their work, build competence, and accept accountability. Great leaders foster self-confidence by believing in their team and offering choices in how to meet goals.

5. ENCOURAGE THE HEART

Leaders encourage the heart to motivate others by recognizing their unique contributions and who they are as individuals. It is crucial to all of us that what we do matters and that our leaders will notice the good work we do and encourage us. It is the little things that often have significant meaning, such as saying thank you, or writing a short note of recognition. Creating a sense of community on teams through celebrations is an essential step in building commitment and social support. Leaders must be present at these events to communicate their gratitude and send a strong message about the value of the contribution.

Katie, a new urgent care director, loved the ideas in the leadership challenge. Her struggle in taking a leadership role was leaving her clinical care comfort zone. She had been an expert clinician for years, but now she felt like a novice in leadership. She spent a great deal of her time with staff in the triage rooms assisting with patient care. Sometimes, she felt like an imposter worrying that she could not live up to others' expectations. In small doses, imposter syndrome is not bad because it reminds us to build our competency. But Katie needs to avoid feeling a high level of self-doubt or a paralyzing fear of failure. It could compromise her ability to be successful. Interestingly, the idea of Katie being an imposter probably never crosses the mind of anyone who works with her.

MOVING FROM AN INDIVIDUAL PERFORMER TO A LEADER

Katie's ambivalence in her leadership role is not unusual. Many nurse leaders achieve promotions because of their excellent clinical and problem-solving skills. They want to continue to add value in this way. This style is a **Superman** approach to leading.[5] You swoop in and fix problems, usually receiving great feedback from staff about how responsive you are. You spend most of your day putting out fires that others bring to your attention. You then find it hard to get your administrative work done because you are available to staff. Over time, this can lead to leadership burnout. You become indispensable, and your team does not grow in their leadership.

A better approach is to be more **Yoda** in your leadership.[5] Yoda is there to coach and support staff but will not solve all their problems.

Yoda is OK with things not being done their way and recognizes that mistakes will be part of the learning. When confronted with issues brought to them by staff, Yoda asks questions that point the staff member in the right direction but does not give them the solution. The Yoda leader can take a day off and not receive fifty texts from staff about what is happening. Yoda recognizes that they should not be indispensable or believe that no one on the unit could take their place if they left.

Becoming more Yoda will help Katie to avoid being a micromanager through her overinvolvement in patient care. Nurse leaders sometimes micromanage their staff because they are more comfortable with clinical decision-making than their leadership responsibilities. When Katie changes her approach, it may not be an easy transition initially for her team. They have become used to Katie jumping in to solve problems and help them with patients. She will need to work hard to empower staff to solve their challenges by asking questions such as:

- What solutions have you already considered?
- What do you think is the right approach?
- What would you do if I were not here?

LEADING FORMER PEERS

Getting promoted from within has always been tricky. You may find yourself leading nurses with much more experience than you have who will question your readiness.[6] Not all your peers will be thrilled with your selection as the leader. While having work experience in an organization when you accept a leadership role is often a tremendous advantage, it can also present some unique challenges. On the positive side, you will not have the steep learning curve about the unit/organizational culture or staff that a leader selected outside the unit might experience. On the negative side, managing former peers when you have been a co-worker can be challenging even when they supported your selection. Your former opinions about unit functioning and your work habits are well known to your co-workers.

In your new leadership role, you need to support and implement decisions made by your organizational leadership. Your relationship with your co-workers will inevitably change as you move from friend and confidant to manager and coach. These changes can lead to awkwardness as you seek a balance in a new and different relationship. There may also be a few staff who do not support your selection and may have even applied for the position themselves. Navigating these dynamics can be challenging. The following are some essential dos and don'ts.

The Dos

1. Meet individually with each staff member regardless of how well you know them. Inquire about their goals and expectations in the same way you would with new staff.
2. Tackle any awkwardness head-on by letting staff know that it can be challenging to switch from peer to nurse leader both for them and for you.
3. Acknowledge the disappointment of staff who may have applied for the role and were not selected.
4. Accept that some staff may decide to transfer or leave the unit because they are not happy with the change, including your selection.
5. Ask for the support of each staff member. Let them know that they are valued and that you need their assistance to be effective in your new role.
6. Talk with staff members that you have had close friendships with about how your relationship may need to change.

THE DON'TS

1. Do not play favorites with former friends. Work to be consistently fair to everyone.
2. Be cautious about socializing with former peers. It is often best to maintain a distance, especially in the initial stages of your transition.
3. Resist taking a patient assignment or getting too involved in clinical care once you have moved into a management role. You will neglect other responsibilities.
4. Do not ignore performance problems in a former peer.
5. Do not immediately de-friend everyone on your Facebook page, but consider transitioning to a professional site that does not include personal information.

Leading former peers takes diplomacy and emotional intelligence. You can be friendly without being a friend. When managed well, a time will come when people forget that you were a peer and see you as their leader.

KEY POINTS

✓ Assuming a leadership role involves developing a new set of role competencies.

✓ Developing a 100-day plan will ensure a smoother role transition.

✓ Frontline leaders are the linchpins in the recruitment and retention of staff.

✓ It is not unusual to feel anxiety and fear of being perceived as an imposter as a new leader.

✓ Leading former peers takes diplomacy and emotional intelligence.

CHAPTER 2

LEADING YOURSELF

Beginning nurse leaders often wonder why there is such a focus during leadership development programs on self-leadership. Why not jump to the core skills needed to be a successful leader, such as budgeting, quality management, and staffing. The answer is evidence-based. When leaders fail, it is rarely because of a lack of knowledge about business skills but rather issues related to their emotional intelligence, or EI. Leadership is an inside-outside process.

Leadership skills begin with understanding one's self. Personal mastery is a critical component of leadership success. Outstanding leaders demonstrate self-confidence and can trust and empower others. They know how their communication and actions impact others and are sensitive to watching the cues in an environment when things are not going well. When you lead, your staff needs to have confidence that you are trustworthy and treat everyone fairly. Leaders make mistakes, but having personal mastery is being able to look at your mistakes, acknowledge them, and learn from them. There is nothing that staff appreciates more than a leader who can say, *I was wrong.* Vulnerability by the leader builds a culture of transparency and psychological safety.

Know Yourself

In 1999, Peter F. Drucker (the father of modern management theory) wrote a classic article for the Harvard Business Review titled *Managing Oneself.* [7] *Drucker* observed that there are few naturally great achievers in life and that most of us will need to learn to manage ourselves to be successful. Here are five strategies to better manage yourself adapted from Drucker's thinking on this subject:

1. **Know your strengths**

   Most people, surprisingly, are not that good at identifying their strengths and weaknesses. There are many ways of identifying our strengths. Some leaders choose to do the Leadership StrengthsFinder 2.0 assessment offered by the Gallup Corporation. [8] After completing the online questionnaire, you will receive a strengths-based leadership report with your five signature strengths. A signature strength is a talent you possess, and if used consistently and productively, it will help you excel. It does not mean that you do not have other strength areas but these five are your strongest. There are different ways to determine your strengths. You can ask trusted colleagues who work with you. You can reflect on things that you do effortlessly, where others might struggle or what brings you the most joy in your work.

2. **Identify how you get things done**

   Nurse leaders often struggle with their workload, bur few take the time to analyze how they get their work done. An important question that every leader needs to ask themselves is: *Am I a reader or a listener?* Leaders need to understand how they best absorb information. Leaders also need to know how they learn best. For example, *do you need to write to clarify a subject,* or *do you want to talk through a problem?* Understanding your work habits is also critical – *do you work better alone or with others? Can you work under stress,* and *do you want to be the decision-maker?*

3. UNDERSTAND YOUR VALUES

Your values should be the ultimate litmus test on whether a job is the right one for you. Do the organization's culture, mission, and strategic direction align with what you believe about your work? They do not need to be precisely the same, but they need to be close enough to co-exist. When your values conflict, it can be impossible to do your best work and support your organization's goals. In Chapter 3, we discuss how to identify your core values.

4. FIGURE OUT WHERE YOU BELONG

Figuring out where you belong in the world can be a challenge. Some roles are a great fit with our strengths and talents; others are not. It is essential to take time to analyze every new position that you are considering. Ask yourself whether the role will play to your unique strengths. Assess whether you will be happy working with the colleagues in this organization or geographic area. It takes courage to decide that what looks like a great promotion will not be the right decision for your career.

5. DECIDE WHAT YOU CAN CONTRIBUTE

A final question that you need to ask yourself is, given your strengths – where can you make the most significant contribution and do your best work? There are many opportunities presented to us throughout our careers, but they will not all be the right ones for us.

Dan reflected on these five strategies when he became unhappy in his role as director of an ambulatory surgical center. He joined the center when it was in a start-up phase. Dan took charge of purchasing much of the equipment and hiring staff. He loved the autonomy and ability to design the processes and procedures. Two years ago, the center was purchased by a large health system. Dan now lacked the independence he once had. His work environment and culture had changed. It was no longer a place where he could make his greatest contribution. It was time for a career pivot. Many elements of our complex and often chaotic health care environment are outside our control. But we can help promote our success as leaders when we do the work we are meant to do.

EMOTIONAL INTELLIGENCE IN LEADERSHIP

Historically, leaders were chosen for their competence and intelligence. But having business smarts is no longer enough. Emotional intelligence is what separates the best from the rest. Our emotional intelligence affects how we manage behavior, negotiate complex social situations, and make decisions. When nurse leaders lack emotional intelligence, it can result in higher staff turnover, reduced engagement, poor relationships with other departments, and an unhealthy work environment.[9] This happened to Emily in her first leadership role. Emily was given an assistant manager position because of her outstanding clinical skills. Problems soon emerged when she became a leader. She used her position power in a punitive way and became defensive when others pointed this out.

Emily's nurse manager coached her using a performance improvement plan that included attending classes on emotional intelligence. Emily took the free online *Do You Lead with Emotional Intelligence* assessment at the beginning of the program.[10] This Harvard Business Review self-assessment evaluates your EI in five key areas of emotional intelligence:

- *Emotional Self-Awareness* – is how well you know your strengths and weaknesses and the impact you have on others.
- *Positivity* – is whether you can maintain a positive outlook in difficult situations.
- *Emotional Self-Control* –is whether you can control impulsive feelings and behaviors.
- *Adaptability* – is whether you are adaptable to frequent changes in the environment.
- *Empathy* – is whether you understand the emotions, needs, and concerns of other people.

Her manager and two peers also took the survey and rated her. Her opportunities for improvement were in emotional self-control, emotional awareness, and empathy. During the EI program, Emily received guidance on how to improve emotional intelligence by doing the following:

1. Seek feedback on your behavior to determine how others are receiving you.
2. Evaluate all negative feedback and reactions to your behavior to look for evidence of where you may have problems with EI.
3. Self-reflect on how you have managed your emotions during a conflict and ask yourself whether there is room for improvement?
4. Assess how you manage your stress level and whether this interferes with relationships with others.
5. Do cognitive rehearsals when confronted with difficult situations to plan how you will manage if you lose control over the situation.

Developing your emotional intelligence takes intentionality. Saying "*This is just who I am*" will not lead to growth. Instead, when you make mistakes, step back, and ask yourself what you will do differently in future situations. Remember, your leadership success is highly dependent on your level of emotional intelligence.

The Introverted Leader

Durante was excited to learn that he'd won the *Leadership Daisy Award* for his hospital. He almost did not apply for a nurse manager role because he was concerned that he was too introverted. He was not sure that he could be an effective leader. His concerns are not unusual among introverts. When we hear about leaders, the descriptions are often about how they are powerful, charismatic, and outgoing. We tend to overvalue extroversion in the United States, often viewing it as a critical leadership quality. Yet, many widely respected current and past world leaders were or are introverts. These include notable individuals such as Albert Einstein, Al Gore, Warren Buffet, Eleanor Roosevelt, Bill Gates, Abraham Lincoln, and Gandhi. Susan Cain is the author of an important book that has achieved international acclaim: *Quiet: The Power of Introverts in a World That Can't Stop Talking.* [11] She contends that introverts are often more creative and careful in their approach to managing problems and risks. Introverts provide important balance in organizations, and there is a need for both introverted and extroverted leaders.

Introversion versus Extroversion

The terms introversion and extroversion are dimensions of personality. *Extroversion* is "the act, state, or habit of being predominantly concerned with obtaining gratification from what is outside the self." Extroverts draw energy from being with others and are prone to boredom when they are by themselves. By contrast, *Introversion* is "the state of or tendency toward being predominantly concerned with and interested in one›s own mental life." Introverts draw energy from being in quiet reflection and lose energy when interacting with large groups of people. These personality dimensions are on a continuum, with some individuals being extremely extroverted, some in the middle, and some very introverted. It can be challenging for extroverts to understand introverts and their need to spend time alone.

STRENGTHS OF INTROVERTED LEADERS

While most leaders tend to be extroverts, many argue that more introverted leaders would better serve today's workplace and workforce because of their high emotional intelligence. Effective leaders should focus on mentoring, empowering, and developing people, behaviors more consistent with introverts than extroverts. Introversion does not mean that a leader is shy, fearful, or unable to act. Instead, it is a way of processing the world and information. Strengths of introverts include the following:

- Introverts think first and talk later.
- Introverts focus on depth rather than superficiality.
- Introverts exude calm.
- Introverts are more comfortable with the written word.
- Introverts are more inclined to empower employees.

THE PITFALLS OF BEING AN INTROVERTED LEADER

Introverted leaders have great strengths but may also have weaknesses that can be pitfalls in a nursing leadership position. Durante learned this on his leadership journey. His need for solitude initially led his staff to think that he was aloof, arrogant, and unfriendly. Although at times it was difficult for him, Durante forced himself to get out of his office several times each day to round with staff, patients, and families. He attended social events for his unit, although sometimes they drained his energy. Durante worked hard to help his team get to know him. He readily shared with the staff that he was introverted. His quiet strength, mentoring, and staff empowerment eventually made him a leader that everyone wanted to work with, as evidenced by his Daisy award.

Avoid Leadership Derailers

Knowing what leadership behaviors to practice is essential. Still, it is equally necessary to consider behaviors that you may exhibit that are not helpful to your team and could cause you to fail. Sometimes our conduct is not addressed in one position but will derail us in another. Here are nine critical suggestions that Marshall Goldsmith, a well-recognized leadership coach, urges leaders to stop doing because they could result in failure or stop your advancement to the next level of leadership:[12]

1. **Adding too much value**

   Nurse leaders sometimes feel compelled to comment on every situation, add their opinions to every conversation, or wordsmith every document they review. Adding too much value is a common problem in leadership. It is a behavior that our co-workers and staff find annoying when done to excess. Simon Senek recommends that leaders learn to talk last in a conversation allowing others to express their viewpoints.[13] Before you say something that you may later regret, ask yourself whether what you are about to say is true, necessary, and strategic?

2. **Passing judgment**

   Many good ideas are never implemented because nurse leaders are too quick to pass judgment on them. Staff will stop offering suggestions if they feel that their leader shuts down the discussion. One way to avoid doing this is to eliminate words like, *however, or but* in conversations. Instead, try what is done in comedy improvisation with the *yes and* approach to keep the conversation flowing. *Yes, and* the new proposal needs to be budget neutral. *Yes, and* we need to do a return on investment before we submit this request.

3. **PASSING THE BUCK**

   Some nurse leaders present changes in policies or procedures as entirely outside of their control, imposed by out-of-touch administrators. There may be a good rationale for changes that are not presented to staff. Interestingly leaders who do this are viewed as being powerless in the eyes of their team.

4. **SPEAKING WHEN ANGRY**

   Emotional volatility is not a useful management tool. Nurse leaders need to control their anger, even in challenging conversations. Leadership reputations can be severely damaged when leaders have an angry emotional response to a situation. It is far better to say nothing or walk away, resuming the conversation when you are less emotional.

5. **WITHHOLDING INFORMATION**

   Some leaders falsely believe that information is power. This power play can work in the short run to maintain an advantage over someone else, but it rarely works in the long run. Withholding information can breed mistrust. In today's environment, our younger generations of nurses look for transparency and want information shared with them. Sharing information will make you a more powerful leader.

6. **FAILING TO GIVE PROPER RECOGNITION**

   Nursing staff wants to be valued for their contributions to the work of the team. When leaders fail to say thank you or take the recognition for themselves, staff feel devalued. Goldsmith observes that successful people become great leaders when they shift the focus from themselves to others.

7. **PLAYING FAVORITES**

   Naturally, nurse leaders may feel closer to some staff than others. What is essential as a leader is to be fair and discourage behaviors that appear to others as "fawning over you" to engender favoritism. Sometimes nurse leaders play favorites with staff who are not their top performers. These actions tilt the field against honest, conscientious employees who will not play along.

8. **Multitasking instead of listening**

   Nurse leaders have incredibly challenging and busy roles. The most passive-aggressive form of disrespect toward a staff member is to continue multitasking (reading email, answering phone calls) during their conversations with you. An interesting thing about listening is that people do not notice when you do it but are certainly aware when you are not listening.

9. **Failing to express gratitude**

   Giving thanks is a magical gesture that some nurse leaders do not use enough. There is nothing more disheartening to staff than to work short-staffed and hear nothing from their leader. An attitude of gratitude is vital in leadership.

As leaders, all of us have things that we do well. But most of us also have annoying habits that we need to stop doing. It is these behaviors that hold us back from being even greater leaders. Take time to review the list above, and honestly ask yourself if there is anything on this list that you need to stop doing.

Nurse Leader Self-Care

Great nurse leaders focus on the needs of others. Unfortunately, in doing so, many put themselves last. Well-being, positivity, health, and happiness are essential for leaders to succeed in today's world. Without a focus on self-care, the stress of the leadership role can easily lead to burnout.[14] This almost happened to Callie. She was anxious to create a good impression during her first six months as a manager. She worked long hours and made herself available 24/7. She was quickly burning out. Callie's director talked with her about the need for self-care and the following four lessons she had learned on her own journey:

1. **REST IS AN INVESTMENT IN YOURSELF,
   YOUR TEAM, AND YOUR FUTURE**
   A lack of rest leads to fatigue, concentration problems, difficulty controlling emotions, and poor decision-making. Leaders experience these problems when they work long hours and stimulate themselves with caffeine to keep going. Caring for self is not selfish behavior on the part of leaders. This investment in rest will make you feel better, be more alert, and better process the many challenges that leaders confront today.

2. **RECHARGING YOUR BATTERY WILL
   MAKE YOU A BETTER LEADER**
   Recharging your battery will both make you a better leader and reduce the likelihood of role burnout. Planning periodic vacations is essential. This recharging of your mind, body, and emotions allows you to be at your best so you can be of service to others. Throughout their careers, nurse leaders learn that life and work move on even in their absence. Wise leaders know that the strongest gauge of their leadership is how well they have developed others to function when they are not there.

3. **FIND AN ACTIVITY OUTSIDE OF WORK
   THAT BRINGS YOU SELF-RENEWAL**
   You should take the time to find at least one activity outside of work that quiets your mind, soothes your soul, and re-energizes you. This activity could be meditation, yoga, walking, reading, cooking, or

prayer. The choice of activity is highly personal. It should be something that enhances your well-being and something you can commit to frequently doing.

4. **LEADERS SET THE EXAMPLE FOR SELF-CARE ON THEIR TEAMS.** In talking with younger nurses, they often tell me that they are concerned about taking leadership positions because they see the imbalance in their own leader's life. Leaders set the example for self-care. If it appears to your staff that self-care and leadership are mutually exclusive from observing your behaviors, this will be the impression they have about leadership roles.

In Chapter 4, we will talk about setting boundaries, which is another aspect of self-care. To achieve a healthy work environment, leaders need to promote self-care. Role modeling is a powerful way to do this. Attention to our self-care will keep us vibrant and establish it as a strong value for our team.

KEY POINTS

✓ Managing yourself is the key to being an effective leader.
✓ Emotional intelligence is more important than IQ when leading others.
✓ Successful leaders avoid career derailers.
✓ Knowing your strengths and talents will make you a better leader.
✓ Good leaders do not have to be extroverts.

CHAPTER 3

BUILDING TRUST AND AUTHENTICITY

N ew nurse leaders are often surprised when the staff does not initially trust them. Yet why should they? Trust builds over time and happens when your team sees consistent behavior, reinforcing that you are trustworthy. In his book *The Speed of Trust*, Stephen M.R. Covey points out that trust is the currency of leadership.[15] When trust is high, things can happen quickly, often at a much lower cost. When trust is low, things happen slowly and cost more. One widely used metaphor to explain trust is viewing it as an emotional bank account (Figure 2). [16]

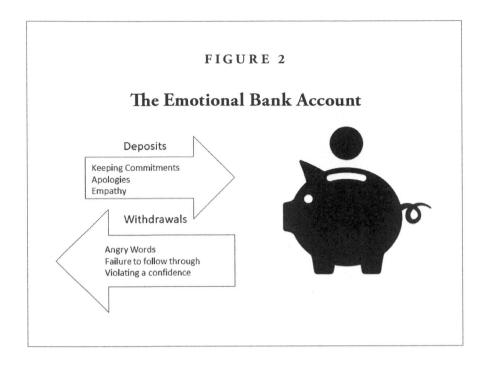

FIGURE 2

The Emotional Bank Account

Deposits

Keeping Commitments
Apologies
Empathy

Withdrawals

Angry Words
Failure to follow through
Violating a confidence

Leaders can either make deposits or withdrawals with their actions. Research from Gallup indicates that to have a high level of trust, leaders need to make six deposits for every withdrawal.[3] Matt, a new leader, lost the trust of his staff during the first few months in his leadership role. He did not answer their emails in a timely way. It often took him up to one week to respond to staff requests. Sometimes, rather than say no to a request, he did not respond at all. In his initial conversations with staff, he talked about his goal to be more supportive than their previous manager. His words did not match his actions. His first three months in the role were rocky until he understood the importance of keeping leadership commitments. He was making lots of withdrawals from an empty bank account. Behaviors that can help build trust more quickly include the following:

1. **Keep your commitments** - This the most significant behavior you can demonstrate. It is the quickest way to build trust in

any relationship. The fastest way to destroy trust is to break commitments or violate promises. Small behaviors like failing to acknowledge an email erode trust.

2. **Extend trust and empower others** – By empowering others, you can leverage your leadership. You should always have a bias, a desire, an inclination to trust people. Assume good intentions. You then create a high-trust culture that brings out the best in nurses and maximizes the team's capability.

3. **Demonstrate integrity** – When you are honest, authentic, and courageous in your actions, you will inspire others' trust. Acknowledge when your behavior has contributed to a problem.

4. **Show a commitment to your work** – Commitment toward a clear purpose is the primary driver of leadership trust. Nurse leaders who believe in their organization's mission, vision, and values and show commitment in their work earn staff trust.

5. **Walk your talk** – Nurses pay much closer attention to what their leaders do versus what they say. Your words and behaviors need to be congruent to be trusted.

6. **Be ethical** – Character and commitment to a deeply held set of values instill trust. When nurse leaders cross ethical boundaries, they are less trusted. Check your facts, do not gossip, and do not trash others who are not in the room.

7. **Strive to be highly competent** – To earn trust, a nurse leader must have some core competence in his/her areas of responsibility. Show up on time to meetings, be prepared, and be ready to work.

8. **Care about your staff** – Nurses want to know that their leaders care about them as people. Be quick to thank others for their work. No one likes to feel like they are not valued. Treat your staff like your moral peers.

9. **Be other-focused – not self-focused** – Words have power in leadership. Staff pay attention to the language that leaders use. Leaders who are self-focused care most about themselves and

strive hard to create a better future for themselves versus their staff. Do not make things about you.

10. **Ask for feedback** – Leaders who ask for feedback demonstrate vulnerability and acknowledge that they are on a journey.

Rebuilding Lost Trust

Sometimes even the best leaders violate trust. Sam is a respected emergency department (ED) director. Candy, one of his seasoned ED nurses, talked with Sam in confidence about her marital problems. He gave her some guidance about employee assistance that was available in their health system. Later that week, a charge nurse reported that Candy had called in sick again. Before thinking about his response, Sam told the charge nurse that Candy was having marital problems. The charge nurse asked Candy about her marital issues later that week.

Candy was devastated that Sam had violated her confidence, and she confronted him. To his credit, Sam immediately apologized to Candy and asked for her forgiveness. He felt terrible about what he had done, although he had not intended to cause harm. He knew that he had withdrawn from the emotional bank account with Candy and would need to make deposits to regain her trust.

Know Your Core Values

To build trust and model the way for others, you need to identify your core values. Joe Tye, an expert on values, reminds us that they should constitute your personal "bottom line" and tell you when to say no and when to say yes.[17] The clearer you are about your values, the easier it will be to stay on your chosen path and commit to it. Finding your voice as a leader better allows you to choose a direction, act with determination, and make the tough choices that come with leadership roles. Examples of core values that some nurse leaders decide to commit to in their practice include the following:

- Evidence-based practice
- Transparency in communication and leadership visibility
- Creation of joy in work
- Shared governance
- Patient safety and quality above all else
- Collaborative practice
- The value of teamwork
- Health equity for all patients
- Diversity on teams
- Customer service
- Tolerance for differences of opinions
- Life-long learning
- Openness to new ideas
- Leadership as service
- Caring-based leadership
- Fairness in all decisions

Clarifying your values as a leader is essential, but staff will watch your behavior to see if you live them. Shared values are very affirming on a team and can lead to exceptional outcomes. Having a strong sense of your core values can also help you decide whether a workplace culture is the right one. Raphael learned this when he took a leadership role in a large physician practice group. Before taking this position, he had worked in large safety-net hospitals that cared for community members irrespective of their ability to pay. He found the physician group members were reluctant to do any pro-bono care or take Medicaid patients in his new role. These policies caused him moral distress because they were not congruent with his core values about health equity and access. He eventually left the position.

Choose a Relational Style of Leadership

Once you identify your core values, the next step is to select a leadership style that reflects what type of leader you hope to become. Relational styles of leadership are grounded in principles that focus on advocacy for staff and building engagement. These approaches improve nursing outcomes and contribute to healthier work environments when compared to more transactional leadership styles.[18] Many nurse leaders have embraced one of the following three relational styles:

Transformational Leadership has been widely adopted in nursing because it is one of the domains in the Magnet Recognition Program ® and leads to the creation of environments that attract and retain nurses.[19] Transformational leaders strive to be both visionary and inspirational. There are four key building blocks to transformational leadership. The first building block is *idealized influence* and describes the leader's ability to both set high standards and serve as a role model for professional practice. The second building block is *inspirational motivation* or the leader's ability to inspire a shared vision that others want to be part of. The third building block is *intellectual stimulation* or the leader's ability to challenge their staff to be creative and innovative while supporting development and growth. The final building block is *individualized consideration* where leaders commit to coaching, mentoring, and an ongoing assessment of staff concerns.

Authentic Leadership is one of the six essential elements in the American Association of Critical Care Nurses' healthy work environment model.[20] It is part of the model because authentic leaders positively affect patient safety, clinical outcomes, and recruitment and retention. Unlike transformational or servant leadership, authentic leadership focuses more on the leader's character and not their charisma or service. Authentic leaders demonstrate self-awareness, a strong ethical compass characterized by moral courage, relational transparency with no hidden agendas, balanced decision-making, and conflict resolution. Openness and honesty are the hallmarks of an authentic leader.

Servant Leadership was popularized by Robert K. Greenfield, who described as servant leader's mindset as one who views themselves as a servant first and leader second.[21] Servant leaders achieve organizational results by attending to the needs of those they serve. The hallmark of a servant leader is their focus on empowering and uplifting those with work with them. They achieve this through active listening, empathy, a focus on healing, emotional intelligence, persuasion, stewardship, a commitment to the individual's growth, and the creation of a sense of community. Servant leaders build psychological safety on their teams, which leads to higher levels of staff engagement.

You may take a leadership role in an organization that advocates for adopting one of the three relational styles and incorporates the principles into their leadership evaluations. That happened when Tamekia became the new director of a hospital-based home care program in a VA Medical Center. During her orientation to the role, she learned that the Department of Veterans Affairs recommends servant leadership as a preferred style for their leaders.[22] Tamekia felt this style was a good fit for her core values. She accepted her role because she believed in the VA's mission and wanted to serve veterans and staff. Servant leadership is a philosophy and practice that emphasizes caring, authenticity and putting Veterans and employees ahead of other goals. Servant Leaders strive to meet both organizational objectives and individual employees' aspirations by encouraging their growth and development. It cultivates capabilities, commitment, and a personal connection to VA's mission. You can make your own decision about which of the three relational styles feels most comfortable for you.

Be a Fire Starter Not a Flame Extinguisher

Once you choose a leadership style, you must walk the talk. You may believe that you are an authentic, servant, or transformational leader, but only your followers can validate this. All three relational leadership styles have a common goal of lighting the fire in staff and not extinguishing the flames of engagement. How do you know if you are a fire starter or a flame extinguisher? The following are some key questions you can ask yourself to determine if you are a fire starter or fire extinguisher:

Fire Starter Behaviors

- Do I show compassion when staff is having challenges in their lives or work?
- Do I focus on the strengths of staff members?
- Do I individualize my leadership to the needs of each staff member?
- Do I encourage innovation?
- Do I help staff grow in place through stretch assignments?
- Do we have a unit or department culture of learning?
- Do I remain optimistic even when times are challenging?
- Do I shine the light on staff achievements?
- Am I passionate, enthusiastic, and engaged in my work?

Fire Extinguisher Behaviors

- Do I blame others for my mistakes?
- Do I feel threatened by high performing staff?
- Do I focus on the weaknesses of staff instead of strengths?
- Do I cut off new ideas by using words like no, but, or however?
- Do I become pessimistic when times are challenging?
- Do I fail to listen to the viewpoints of others?
- Do I believe staff is lucky to have jobs?

- Do I fail to give others a second chance?
- Do I think staff should leave personal problems at home?
- Do I withhold information that others need to do their work?
- Am I unapproachable or not visible on the unit?
- Do I lack passion or engagement in my work?

Fire starters are leaders with relational styles who coach and mentor others. Fire extinguishers tend to be transactional in their work, cause stress, and lead staff to disengage. Which one would you rather work for?

KEY POINTS

✓ Trust is the currency of leadership.
✓ Rebuilding lost trust quickly is vital in leadership.
✓ Knowing your core values will help guide your choices in leadership.
✓ Relational leadership styles are linked to better patient outcomes and healthier work environments.
✓ Be a fire starter and not a fire extinguisher in your leadership.

CHAPTER 4

ORGANIZING YOUR WORK

Frontline nurse leaders feel pulled in many directions in their work. Deciding what is essential and where to spend your time and energy can be challenging. Many leaders describe their roles as feeling like the monkey in the middle. Above you are layers of organizational leaders, and below you are the staff. Figure 3 illustrates the types of expectations your organization's administrative leaders may have compared with those of your team.

FIGURE 3

Leaders are Pulled in Many Directions

Organizational Leadership
- You will run operations.
- You will conserve resources.
- You will satisfy patients.
- You will implement change.
- You will meet metrics.
- You will promote quality.
- You will ensure safety.

Staff Expect
- You will advocate for them.
- You will coach them.
- You will care about their needs.
- You will provide the resources needed.
- You will keep them safe.
- You will develop them.

SET WORK BOUNDARIES

A healthcare environment is a noisy place. When you are in a leadership role, there are many demands on your time, from hundreds of email messages a day to back-to-back organizational meetings. Carving out time to accomplish all your administrative responsibilities can be daunting. When Sophia accepted the role of director of pediatrics and women's health in a large medical center, she did not anticipate how much her workload would expand from her previous role as a unit manager. She had learned to achieve work-life balance as a manager but now found herself less successful juggling all her new responsibilities. Her task list became longer every day. Initially, her solution was simply to work more hours, but she soon found herself working more than sixty hours each week, which left her exhausted and unable to spend quality time with her family. She was now in overdrive and needed to set boundaries in her work.

Setting boundaries in our work can help us control of our lives. Making decisions about where we invest our time, our work hours and what we should delegate helps us to preserve our physical and emotional energy and identify our limits. [23] The following are four critical steps in setting your boundaries:

1. **Identify your limits** – We are often our own worst enemies when it comes to working. You may have challenges saying no. Getting clear about your emotional, mental, physical, and spiritual limitations is an essential first step. Acknowledging our limits helps guide us to know when we are stepping over lines and moving into destructive patterns. Limitations are a very individual thing and may vary considerably among leaders.

2. **Pay attention to your feelings** – Feelings are a good gauge of whether we have moved into overdrive with our work. Pay close attention when you feel discomfort, resentment, or guilt about work. These feelings can signal that a boundary issue may be present. If you think these feelings repeatedly, then it is time to restructure your boundaries.

3. **Permit yourself to set boundaries** – Nurse leaders often feel that they should be able to cope with challenging work situations and time constraints. Sometimes, their immediate supervisor may see the leader working long hours and say nothing. Leader boundaries are something that you have the right to set. If you do not set limits, you will feel drained and overextended at best and resentful at worst. When these doubts occur, reaffirm that you do indeed have this right, permit yourself to do so, and work to preserve them. Plan a time to leave work every day and stick to it except in cases of extreme emergencies. Be clear with the staff about boundaries involving texts and emails in the evenings and on weekends.

4. **Consider your environment** – Work environment context plays a crucial role in how comfortable leaders may be in setting boundaries. Your environment can either support your

setting boundaries making it easier for you or present obstacles to boundary setting making it more challenging for you. That is why nurse executives play such a key role in making it OK for their leaders to set boundaries.

Determine What Matters Most

Sometimes nurse leaders describe their workload management challenges as time management problems. Yet, there will never be enough time unless you are very disciplined in what you say yes to and when you say no. Most leaders keep long task lists of goals they want to accomplish. When we create these task lists, we can think that everything matters equally, but the truth is that it does not. Success is sequential, not simultaneous. It is one step at a time. In his book *The One Thing: The Surprising Simple Truth Behind Extraordinary Results*, Gary Keller suggests that we should focus on the one thing right now that will matter most. [24] This one thing may not be your only thing on a to-do list, but it is the *one thing* right now.

Keller is a firm believer in the Pareto principle, or the 80/20 law of the vital few. This principle has research support. The rule proposes that a minority (20%) of actions, inputs, and efforts lead to most of the results, outputs, or rewards. In other words, a small amount of effort in the right areas can lead to the most significant outcomes. You need to look for an action that has a domino effect. Trying to multitask and make many things happen at once is overrated in terms of effectiveness. Ask yourself, *"What is the one thing that would have the most significant payback for me?"* When Sophia asked herself this, she discovered that developing the leaders who reported to her would be the one thing she could do that would matter most in her role. With this development, she could begin to delegate some of her responsibilities to others on her team. I often ask new nurse leaders about their *one* thing that would have the greatest payback for them if they invested in doing it. The following are some of the answers that they have given me:

- Conduct leadership rounds more regularly.
- Create a process for tracking four to six critical performance metrics.
- Spend more time coaching staff.
- Develop the leadership skills of charge nurses.
- Become more approachable.
- Schedule set times to read email.
- Structure communication methods on the unit.
- Talk less and listen more.
- Learn to read and develop a budget.
- Become more proficient with technology.
- Set boundaries around work and leave the unit by 5 p.m.

When leaders ask themselves the question, they are almost always accurate. Most nurse leaders instinctively know what matters most. It is taking the next step that becomes important, which means going small for the fewer things that will have the most effect.

Avoid Meeting Fear of Missing Out (FOMO)

New leaders are often inundated with requests to attend numerous meetings in their organizations. Without triaging these requests, it is easy to become overwhelmed, trying to be "everywhere." That is where Keven found himself after six months in a leadership role. He was having trouble getting his administrative work done because of the time spent in meetings. Often the meetings did not seem related to issues involving his unit. Like many beginning leaders, Kevin mistakenly believed that the only way he could stay in his organization's loop was to attend all the scheduled meetings.

His mentor suggested that he give up feelings of FOMO and break his addiction to meeting attendance. She recommended that he needed to consider whether he needed to be there before attending any meeting. His mentor reminded him that taking the time to participate in a meeting meant he would not be doing something else in his administrative area of responsibility. He learned to request the agenda in advance and decide whether he needed to attend all, part, or none of the meeting.

There are nurse leaders who measure their value by how many meetings they attend. They feel insulted when they are not in the loop on everything. While going to many meetings may make you feel important, it is not the right strategy to allocate your time.[25] You need to permit yourself to decline meetings.

LEADER ROUNDING

One evidence-based activity essential to incorporate into your work schedule if you are in an inpatient leadership role is leader rounding. Leader rounds on patients has quickly become a best practice in hospitals throughout the United States. When done well, it can have a positive direct impact on both patients and staff satisfaction.[26] It is an organized way for nurse leaders to be visible. Purposeful rounding can lead to conversations that will build trust and facilitate communication. As a leader, you will learn what is working well on your unit or department and where improvement is needed. The following five key steps are ways to make your rounding more purposeful:

1. BE CONSISTENT

Effective leadership rounding begins with a planned schedule of when you will round. Many health care organizations provide leaders specific guidance about when to do rounding. If your organization does not, you need to establish your own plan. Ideally, you should round on every inpatient during the first 24 to 48 hours after admission to the unit. Your goal should be to see each patient at least once during their hospitalization. Blocking out the time to do this in your daily schedule is essential. Plan on 60-90 minutes at a time when you are least likely to interrupt care or treatment routines. These visits will typically take between five and ten minutes but may take longer if the patient has concerns that you need to address.

2. ESTABLISH KEY QUESTIONS THAT YOU ASK OF EVERY PATIENT/FAMILY

There is no better way to find out about the care that patients receive on your unit than to ask them. Structuring the conversation is crucial because it will help you stay on track and find out the information you need.[27] The following is a sample script used in many organizations:

- Good morning (or afternoon), my name is _____, and I am the nurse manager on this unit. I am visiting you today because I am interested in finding how about your hospital stay. Would you mind answering a few questions?
- I see your nurse is _____ She/he is excellent, and they will take good care of you.
- Is our staff responding to your call bells and checking in to see if you need anything?
- Are we managing your pain appropriately?
- Do you have any concerns that you would like to discuss with me?
- Is there anything I can do for you right now to make you more comfortable? I have the time.
- Give the patient your business card and contact number.

3. FOLLOW UP QUICKLY ON IDENTIFIED PROBLEMS

While rounding on patients, you should look for opportunities for immediate service recovery. A nurse manager told me a story about rounding on a quite upset patient about a test delay. She noticed that the patient had no cards, flowers, or visitors at the bedside, although she had been in the hospital for three days. The manager went down to the gift shop and bought a small plant for the patient. *"The patient was so appreciative"*, she told me. *"It was clear to me that she was all alone in this experience. The key to service recovery is to ask yourself what great would look like in this situation."*

4. RECOGNIZE THE WORK OF STAFF AS YOU ROUND

Nurse leader rounding on patients is also an excellent opportunity to interact with staff and listen to their concerns. Leaders should scan the environment for equipment and supply issues that concern staff. Before rounding, ask staff if there is anything that you should know about their patients. With new graduates, ask them about what their challenges are in managing complex patients. Follow-up with any concerns after your rounding. Always convey any compliments about the staff received from patients.

5. TRACK TRENDS IN PATIENT COMMENTS/ QUESTIONS/PATIENT BEHAVIOR

Many organizations use standardized rounding sheets to track patient comments and concerns. Use patient rounding to look for trends in the population that you are serving that can be helpful in strategic planning. One nurse leader told me that her patients were asking about the availability of iPads, which later led to the hospital installing iPads in patient rooms – a big satisfier. Another nurse leader shared with me that she could see that a growing number of her patients were Spanish speaking from her rounding. She advocated for her organization to provide a Spanish class for health care providers.

Often, it is the simple things like leadership rounding that can lead to substantial improvements in the quality of care and staff satisfaction. Although purposeful nurse leader rounding is a considerable time commitment, most nurse leaders will also tell you that it is the best part of their day. There is nothing more satisfying than to hear that your staff are doing a great job. It helps you keep a line of sight to the patient that is critical for your satisfaction and engagement.

NURSE LEADER VISIBILITY

You cannot successfully lead nursing staff if you are not visible and accessible. Janet, a surgical services leader, was disappointed with the quarterly Glint staff engagement findings from her units. Janet was responsible for overseeing two clinical areas with more than 100 nursing staff. Her leadership rounding was inconsistent. A frequent comment from the teams on both units was that she was not visible.

Janet's challenge is not unique in today's environment. The dilemma is, which we know from generational research, that younger Millennial and Generation Z nurses want leaders who are accessible to them and will coach them. They often have little understanding of the broad scope of the manager's responsibilities. No one wants to be led by someone who rarely, if ever, comes out of their office—visibility in leadership matters. Wise leaders work to incorporate visibility into their daily routines using strategies such as leader rounding, attendance at shift huddles, and an open office door for at least part of the day.

During times of crisis, leader visibility is even more essential. No matter how challenged you are for time, you cannot lead from behind the desk. You must make time to be visible, to be seen, and to listen.

LEARN TO SAY NO

Your time is a limited commodity. Every time you commit to something, it will leave less time for other activities. The more successful you are in a leadership career, the less accessible you will become. A leader cannot be equally available to all people. You are often faced with the dilemma of who gets your time and who does not. Requests for your time are, in a sense, an affirmation that you are successful in your work. While this can be very flattering, you can also quickly burn out from becoming over-committed. Learning to say no to more requests can be one of the biggest favors you can do yourself and those you love. It helps reduce stress levels and gives you time for what is important.

When you say no to a new commitment, you are honoring your existing obligations. You are also ensuring that you will be able to devote quality time to them. Despite knowing this, it can be difficult for leaders to say no. You may worry that you are missing out on a great opportunity. It is important to remember that saying no may give you time for different options that may be more important, personally or professionally. Here are some statements that you can use to say no in a positive way.[28]

- *I would love to be involved, but I cannot commit to this as I have other priorities.*
- *Now's is not a good time as I am in the middle of something else. I may be able to do this at another time.*
- *I am not the best person to help you with this. Why don't you try (offer a suggestion)?*
- *This sounds like an exciting opportunity, but no, I cannot do it.*

Most of us have also found ourselves in situations where we said yes reluctantly and later regretted our decision. Some people will be pushy, so you need to learn to be firm but polite in your choices. If you allow it, others' priorities could crowd out time you have to spend with your family and close friends. Do not leave the door open for further negotiation. You may find yourself saying no to good things to focus on higher priorities. Saying no may also allow you to try new things. If you have volunteered for five years to chair a heart walk, it may be time to give someone else the opportunity. It is essential to recognize that your resources are finite to avoid the guilt trap. Saying no is about respecting and valuing your time and space. If done well, people may not be happy with your refusal, but they will understand.

KEY POINTS

✓ Deciding what is essential and where to spend your time and energy in a leadership role can be particularly challenging.

✓ Setting boundaries helps protect us, clarify our responsibilities, preserve our physical and emotional energy, stay focused on ourselves, live our values and standards, and identify our limits.

✓ A small amount of effort in the right areas can lead to the most significant outcomes.

✓ Purposeful rounding is an organized way for nurse leaders to be visible.

✓ Every time you commit to something, it will leave less time for other activities, so learn to say no.

CHAPTER 5

IMPROVING YOUR DECISION-MAKING SKILLS

Nurse leaders make many decisions in their daily work. Some choices are so routine that we can make them with minimal deliberation, but others demand more reflective and critical thinking. In ambiguous situations such as the experience with COVID-19, decisions needed to be made rapidly, often without complete information. Some leaders feel confident that they can quickly arrive at the best solutions based on their education and experience. They pride themselves on their decisiveness. Other leaders deliberate even small decisions for extended periods, which can be frustrating for their staff. Jeff Bezos, the CEO at Amazon, talks about the need to separate decisions into two categories.[29] The first is what he calls the one-way door. These are decisions that are irreversible and highly consequential such as a decision to leave an organization. These decisions demand a high level of deliberation. Most of our decisions fall into a second category which Bezos describes as two-way door decision. You can make a wrong two-way door decision and then backup and reverse course. What is key is to know what decision-making category you are in when deciding.

Most leaders have made at least one decision in their careers that they later regretted. Often the decisions that we regret are made without the best evidence available or the right stakeholder input. Sometimes leaders fail to consider the impact of their decision on the rest of the system. The ramifications of important decisions often have a ripple effect on other departments and sometimes unintended consequences. Like clinical practice, which should be evidence-based, decision making should also be informed by evidence from stakeholders, the leader's experience, and organizational evidence.[30]

New leaders like Allan sometimes learn the hard way what happens if you fail to consider all the evidence. Only six weeks into his role, Allan was asked by an orthopedic surgeon if he could change his regularly scheduled OR day from Tuesday to Monday. Allan took a quick look at the OR schedule and said he did not see a problem with the request. He committed to making the scheduling change the following month. With the decision made, the orthopedic surgeon began scheduling his patients. Allan later found out that his health system had purchased an orthopedic group. Their practice agreement guaranteed that they could do their cases on Mondays. Allan could not accommodate their schedule and that of the other orthopedic surgeon. He learned the following five lessons from this experience:

1. He had framed the request as being a minor decision when it was much more complicated.
2. He had failed to critically analyze all the potential implications and consequences of the change.
3. He had not consulted other critical stakeholders in his organization for their input on the request's feasibility.
4. He had limited himself to the one decision option.

5. He had committed to a plan that he could not execute, placing his organization at financial risk from the possible loss of the surgeon's business.

EXPAND YOUR DECISION OPTIONS

In the situation above, Allan had limited his decision options to just one. Like Allan, leaders often fail to consider a range of options when deciding. Many leaders look at the information in front of them and trust their guts too much in making decisions. The solution to better decision-making is to broaden your thinking. The WRAP model developed by Chip and Dan Heath is one strategy you can use to expand your decision-making.[31] It is a process that includes the following steps:

Widen your options - In our decision-making, we often turn our choices into either/or without expanding our options. The Heaths suggest that you ask yourself the question, *If I could not choose either one of these options, what else would I do?* This will help to avoid narrowing your options.

Reality test your assumptions - Many of us regularly consult rating sites such as Amazon, Trip Advisor, or Yelp before buying a product, using a hotel, or visiting a restaurant. Unfortunately, we do not always test our assumptions in the same way in our leadership roles. We need to seek and listen closely to alternate opinions. Unit practice councils can often provide excellent reality checks about decisions for nurse leaders.

Attain distance before deciding - We are often easily influenced by what feels familiar to us, and we avoid loss aversion. If it is a critical decision, ask yourself how you will think about a potential choice in ten minutes, ten months, and ten years. Always honor your core values and priorities.

Prepare to be wrong - Even when taking the three above steps, not every decision you make will be the right one. Wise leaders know that it is best to be transparent when deciding, especially during turbulent times. You make the decision based on the best evidence that you have today. We all do need to prepare to be wrong about some of the decisions we make today.

Having a process to help you in your decision making is essential. Pay close attention to information that does not confirm your opinion. Look for alternate ways to frame the problem. Be prepared to act if things go unexpectedly well or poorly. The WRAP process does not guarantee a good outcome. But it sets guardrails to keep you from falling into the common decision-making traps.

Avoid Decision Biases

We often think narrowly about our decisions and do not develop systematic approaches to compare our choices. A failure to broaden our options can be an outcome of cognitive or decision biases.[32] These are mental shortcuts that we take in our thinking or filters we use in evaluating situations. An awareness of your potential biases can lead you to ask better questions and avoid autopilot decision-making. Common decision biases seen in healthcare environments include the following:

Sunk cost bias - When we are heavily invested in a project or initiative, it is hard to pull back because of the investments that we have already made. It can push us to do things that we should not do because we are loss averse. It is why investors hang onto stocks much longer than they should. It is also why some couples stay in relationships for years when divorce might have been the better option. Letting go is challenging when we have invested emotional energy, time, money, and other resources.

We overlook the reality that a decision to continue a project also costs time and resources, limiting investment in other initiatives. Sometimes this bias is driven by ego, not wanting to acknowledge that the original decision, while OK at the time, is no longer a good one.

Confirmation bias - As leaders, we feel more comfortable with people who value what we value and agree with our opinions. Confirmation bias is when we only seek views that agree with ours and avoid those that threaten our world view. This decision trap can happen if we do not routinely ask others to pushback on our decisions and point out the downsides.

Observational bias - Observational selection bias is when we start noticing things that we did not see before but wrongly assume that the frequency has increased. Nurse leaders sometimes do this when a problem is brought to them involving a staff member. They begin paying close attention and can mistakenly believe that the behavior occurs more often than it does leading the employee to feel that they are being "singled out."

Status quo bias - In our changing health care environment, the status quo can feel comfortable. The status quo bias is when we believe that most change would be for the worse, and we stick to our routines and ways of doing things. Our decisions then tend to be in the direction of maintaining the status quo versus trying anything new or different.

Projection bias - Projection bias is when we believe that others agree with us on issues. We fail to ask if there is disagreement. The danger here is that we can assume a consensus on issues when there is none. Leaders may feel blindsided when a decision made turns out to be highly unpopular when they believed there was agreement.

Bandwagon effect bias - The bandwagon effect bias occurs in settings with a groupthink mentality. This bias happens in strong cultures where individuals adopt a set of norms and conform. Unfortunately, it can lead to flawed thinking and poor decision-making because of an unwillingness to consider alternative information. The worldview of the group may not be that of the larger society.

The most effective way to avoid bias in your thinking is to encourage others to challenge your opinions and ideas. Your best decision-making will occur when you have considered all aspects of a situation, including those that might be uncomfortable. Easy solutions and quick decisions are not always the best. We need to strive to see more nuances in decisions by being aware of our biases.

SEEK FEEDBACK

Your decision-making skills will improve if you are open to the feedback of others. Brooke, a nurse residency program director, was concerned that so many new graduates who accepted positions at her medical center resigned to return to graduate school after their first year in practice. She frequently complained about this trend in meetings with the nursing executive leadership team. Her chief nursing officer challenged her to think differently about the new graduate transition program observing that she had fallen into confirmation bias with no real plans to change the status quo. The CNO observed that Brooke was in a great position to build content into her one-year program to expand the new graduates' decision-making options. After their discussion, Brooke recognized that she had become complacent and accepted the status quo.

It can be challenging in nurse leader roles to get direct feedback, but it is critical. Setting up a feedback culture should begin with the leader modeling behavior that values input and minimizes defensive responses. When you have a track record of accepting personal accountability using the "I" word, staff will feel more comfortable giving you feedback. While positive feedback is excellent, much of our most significant growth will come with suggestions to improve our performance. The following are three key questions you can use to elicit specific feedback:

1. What should I **keep** doing as a leader because it supports the team and leads to good outcomes?
2. What should I **start** doing in my leadership role to support our team efforts and achieve better outcomes?
3. What should I **stop** doing in my leadership role to better support the team and achieve better outcomes?

You will not always agree with the feedback that you receive. In some situations, you may need to let the person know that they are entitled to their opinions, but that you disagree with their assumptions. But sometimes, there is truth in these observations. When you receive feedback, change your mental model from viewing it as criticism to seeing it as a gift with data that you did not have before allowing you to make more informed decisions in the future.

Be Reflective

Most nurse leaders have such busy lives that they leave little time for reflection about their daily work. Sean found himself in this situation. He took a director role in an urgent care center, feeling proud that he had fast-tracked his leadership career. Within a few weeks, he realized that the center's problems were more serious than those discussed with him during his interview. The medical director of the clinic was a bully, and acceptance of his behavior was part of the organizational culture. Sean now had serious misgivings about his ability to improve the center's culture without a more substantial organizational commitment.

His solution was to stay in motion and keep putting out the fires even though he was not making progress.

Sean's situation is not unusual. Real learning from our experiences requires reflection. Until we reflect on our behaviors and actions, we may not develop the new insights needed that might lead us to act differently in the future. Gaining wisdom from any experiences, especially the unsuccessful ones, takes reflection. Instead of constant acceleration, we need to, at times, just stop and think. Sean contacted a mentor who advised him to reflect for a few days about his situation, then they would discuss some of his lessons learned. After thinking about the whole experience, he identified the following key learnings:

1. He had jumped at an opportunity to serve as director of the urgent care center without doing the due diligence needed to assess if it was a good fit.
2. He had been flattered that others felt he could improve a culture when previous leaders had been unsuccessful.
3. He had not sought out the guidance of mentors who had been helpful to him in the past.
4. He was naïve in workplace politics and his ability to pick up the clues that the culture was toxic.

These were significant insights for a young leader on his career journey. It is crucial to examine events and ask ourselves how they have shaped the way we see the world, others, and ourselves. The act of reflection can help build our resiliency. It offers us the opportunity to go back and think through what we would do the next time instead of ruminating about our actions and decision outcomes. It is proactive versus reactive thinking and helps us to do more proactive reflective thinking in the future. Some important questions to ask yourself about your decisions include the following:[33]

- What was my process for making this decision? Did I seek input, use intuition, consult data, etc.?
- How quickly was I able to decide? What factors influenced the speed of my decision?
- How did it impact the livelihood, emotions, work environment, or success of others?
- What was the ripple effect of my actions or inaction?
- Overall, how do I feel about the decision? Would I make it again? What would change?

Some leaders, especially in the early stages of a new role, have found reflective journaling helpful. The act of writing down your ideas can help to clarify thinking. Experts at the Center for Creative Leadership offer some valuable guidance on how to do this.[34] They recommend using the following format to evaluate experiences that may be shaking your equilibrium.

- **The event or experience** – Describe it as objectively as possible, sticking to the facts. *Who was involved? Where did it happen? When did it happen?*
- **Your reaction** – Describe your response as factually and objectively as possible. *What did you do? What were your thoughts? What were your feelings?*
- **The lessons** – Evaluate what you learned from both the event and from your reaction to it. *Did the event suggest a personal development need that you should address? Do you see a pattern in your responses?*

Increasingly, we see reflection as part of leadership competency models. Your leadership experiences are only as valuable as what you do with them, and this requires reflection.

KEY POINTS

✓ Most decisions that we later regret are made without the best evidence available or the right stakeholder input.

✓ Leaders often fail to consider a range of options when deciding.

✓ An awareness of your potential biases can lead you to ask better questions and avoid autopilot decision-making.

✓ Your decision-making skills will improve if you are open to the feedback of others.

✓ Reflection allows us to think through what we would do differently instead of ruminating about our actions or decision outcomes.

Part 1 References

1. Warshawsky N, Cramer E. Describing nurse manager role preparation and competency findings from a large study. *Journal of Nursing Administration.* 2019; 49(5); 249-255.
2. Saifman H, Sherman R. The experience of being a Millennial nurse manager. *Journal of Nursing Administration.* 2019; 49(7/8); 366-371.
3. Clifton J, Harter J. *It's the Manager.* New York: Gallup Press; 2019.
4. Kouzes J, Posner B. *The Leadership Challenge 6th Edition.* San Francisco: Jossey-Bass; 2017.
5. Raymond, J. (Interview Huffington Post April 27th, 2017 blog). Dear Boss: Be More like Yoda, Less Like Superman. Available at https://www.huffpost.com/entry/dear-boss-be-more-like-yod a-less-like-superman_b_590252a8e4b05279d4edba5e
6. Moyo M. Millennial nurse manager: Leading staff nurses more experienced than you. *Nurse Leader.* 2019; 17(3); 253-256.
7. Drucker PF. Managing oneself. *The Harvard Business Review.* 1999; 77(2), 64-74, 185.
8. Rath T, Conchie B. *Strengths Based Leadership: Great Leaders, Teams, and Why People Follow Them.* New York: Gallup Press; 2008.

9. Coladonato A, Manning ML. Nurse leader emotional intelligence: How does it affect clinical nurse job satisfaction. *Nursing Management.* 2017; 48(9); 26-32.

10. McKee, A. (June 5, 2015 Harvard Business Review Blog). Quiz yourself: Do you lead with emotional intelligence. Available at https://hbr.org/2015/06/quiz-yourself-do-you-lead-with-emotional-intelligence

11. Cain S. *Quiet: The Power of Introverts in a World That Can't Stop Talking.* New York: Crown Publishers; 2013.

12. Goldsmith M. *What Got You Here Won't Get You There.* New York: Hyperion; 2007.

13. Sinek S. *Leaders eat Last: Why some Teams pull Together and Others Don't.* New York: Portfolio; 2017.

14. Kelly LA., Lefton C, Fischer SA. Nurse leader burnout, satisfaction, and work-life balance. *Journal of Nursing Administration.* 2019; 49(9); 404-410.

15. Covey SMR. *The Speed of Trust: The One Thing that Changes Everything.* New York: Free Press; 2018.

16. Covey SR. *The 7 Habits of Highly Effective People 30th Anniversary Edition.* New York: Simon & Schuster; 2020.

17. Tye J. Living your values. *Nurse Leader.* 2020; 18(1); 67-72.

18. Wei H, King A, Jiang Y, Sewell KA, Lake D. The impact of nurse leadership styles on nurse burnout: A systematic review of the literature. *Nurse Leader.* 2020; 18(5); 439-450.

19. American Nursing Credential Center. *The Magnet Model.* Available at https://www.nursingworld.org/organizational-programs/magnet/magnet-model/

20. American Association of Critical-Care Nurses. *Healthy Work Environment Standards.* Available at https://www.aacn.org/nursing-excellence/healthy-work-environments

21. Greenfield RK., Spears LC. *Servant Leadership: A Journey into the Nature of Legitimate Power and Greatness 25th Anniversary Edition.* Mahwah NJ: Paulist Press; 2002.

22. Mustard RW. Servant leadership in the Veterans Health Administration. *Nurse Leader. 2020;* 18(2); 178-180.

23. Gionta DW, Guerra D. *From stressed to centered: A practical guide to a happier and healthier you.* Santa Barbara: Sea Hill Press; 2015.

24. Keller G, Papasan J. *The One Thing: The Surprising Simple Truth Behind Extraordinary Results.* Austin, TX.: Bard Press; 2013.

25. Saunders EB. (February 26, 2013 Harvard Business Review Blog*).* Break your Addiction to Meetings. Available at https://hbr.org/2013/02/break-your-addiction-to-meetin

26. Blake PG., Bacon CT. Structured rounding to improve staff satisfaction with leadership. *Nurse Leader.* 2020; 18(5), 461-466.

27. Studer Group. *The Nurse Leader Handbook: The Art and Science of Nursing Leadership.* Pensacola, FL: The Studer Group; 2019.

28. Ury W. *The Power of the Positive No: Save the Deal, Save the Relationship and Still Say No.* New York: Bantam Books; 2007.

29. Bezos J. *Invent and Wander: The Collected Writings of Jeff Bezos.* Harvard Business Review Press; 2021.

30. Majors SM, Warshawsky N. Evidence-based decision making for nurse leaders. *Nurse Leader.* 2020, 18(5). 471-475.

31. Heath C., Heath D. *Decisive: How to make better decisions in Life and Work.* New York: Crown Books; 2013.

32. Mindtools. Avoiding psychological biases in decision making: How to make objective decisions. Available at https://www.mindtools.com/pages/article/avoiding-psychological-bias.htm

33. Donahue B. (Smart Brief Leader Blog November 6th, 2020). Mining your leadership story. Available at https://www.smartbrief.com/original/2020/11/mining-your-leadership-story

34. Center for Creative Leadership. Leadership resilience: Handling stress, uncertainty, and setbacks. Available at https://www.ccl.org/articles/leading-effectively-articles/leadership-resiliency-handling-stress-uncertainty-and-setbacks/

PART 2

COMMUNICATING AND COLLABORATING IN LEADERSHIP ROLES

"The way we communicate with others ultimately determines the quality of our lives."

TONY ROBBINS

CHAPTER 6

MASTERING COMMUNICATION

As a leader, you are always communicating. It is an essential leadership skill because of the impact excellent communication can have on productivity, quality, morale, and retention. Communication can be challenging in healthcare, where large spans of control are typical, and staff work 24/7 in many settings. Some messages can be challenging to communicate positively. With four generations in the nursing workforce, there are generational differences in how staff prefer to receive communication. Not surprisingly, breakdowns in communication play a significant role in problems that occur in healthcare settings.

New leaders are often surprised at how many times they need to communicate the same message. Messages are rarely received and completely understood the first time they are shared. It is not a one-and-done activity. Marketing experts recommend using *"the rule of seven"* based on research that it can take up to seven times for an audience to act on a message.[1] You should also plan to use three or more channels to communicate important information. These channels can include team huddles, communication boards, newsletters, group text messages, emails, a unit Facebook page, or a staff meeting. Storytelling is powerful in leadership. If you present changes in policies or practices, stories are an excellent way to convey the why behind messages and reconnect staff to their purpose.

Although our focus is often on verbal communication skills, leaders communicate in the following four different ways:

Verbal – the words that you use and how you structure your messages.

Non-verbal – your body language including gestures, facial expressions, eye contact.

Para-verbal – the tone, pacing and pitch of your voice.

Digital presence – your communication digitally on email, texts, and social media.

Staff observe all four aspects of your communication. Sandy learned early in her leadership that she needed to ensure that her non-verbal communication matched the messages she was trying to send. On a yearly employee satisfaction survey, many on her staff noted that she often had an angry expression on her face and rarely smiled. She was viewed as unapproachable even though that was not her intent. As a leadership development goal, she began to work on her non-verbal body language using a trusted peer to give her feedback on her progress. Beginning leaders often struggle with their communication. It is helpful to ask a trusted peer to observe you when you communicate and give you feedback.

Styles of Communication

All of us have different preferred styles of communication. While it may be more comfortable communicating with others who have a similar style to our own, this is not an option in a leadership role where you need to flex your style to meet others' needs. The following are four different styles of communication you will encounter in your leadership role:[2]

The first style is the *analyzer*. Analyzers are persuaded by facts and data versus emotion and story. Staff with an analyzer communication style usually prefer not to engage in a great deal of small talk. They are often more introverted, highly organized, and value accuracy. When working with team members who have this communication style, keep your conversations short, and directly come to the point in your discussions. Do not get upset if there not a great deal of sharing of personal information or if you get closely questioned about decisions that you have made.

Another communication style you will find on your team is *relator*. Relators are people oriented. They are generally warm, friendly, and nurturing individuals who highly value interpersonal relationships. Unlike analyzers, relators want you to take an interest in them as people. They are ideal team players because they enjoy teamwork. When working with relators, show a sincere interest in them as people. Engage in small talk before you move to requests. Be predictable, and honor promises you make.

A third communication style you will encounter is that of *director*. Staff with a director style are driven by a need to get things done. A director style of communication tends to be fast-paced and goal-oriented. Many in leadership have this style because it is a natural go-getter mentality. When communicating with directors, be clear, brief, and precise. Skip the small talk and avoid too much detail. If you do not have this style yourself, do not get offended by what you might perceive as impatience or insensitivity.

The last style of communication that you will encounter is the *socializer.* Socializers are charismatic and have high energy levels. They love working on teams and building relationships with others. When communicating with socializers, take the time to build a relationship and socialize with them. Your directions should be clear about what needs to happen and a timeline as they are less attentive to time. Socializers take criticism personally, so avoid being too critical and use motivating language.

Taking the time to understand your staff's communication styles and those of other leaders will help you meet their needs more effectively. Dana learned this when her relationship with a new CNO became contentious. Dana's style of communicating was that of an analyzer. She directed her medical center's infection prevention program. The new CNO was a relator who highly valued interpersonal relationships. Dana had made it clear in their first few encounters that she was not interested in small talk. The CNO had become offended and talked with Dana about her abrupt approach in dealing with others. They agreed that they would both take a communication style inventory. [3] Once they gained awareness of each other's style, both tried to flex to each other's needs.

THE HEART – HEAD – HANDS APPROACH

The conventional pathway that the leaders use when presenting communication about change starts with what and then explains how. This approach does not work with younger staff. They need to understand the why behind a change before moving to the how and later the what (Figure 4). This is sometimes called the Heart – Head – Hands approach to communication.

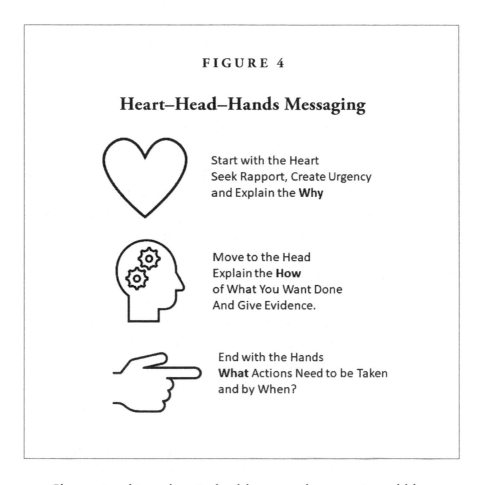

FIGURE 4

Heart–Head–Hands Messaging

Start with the Heart
Seek Rapport, Create Urgency
and Explain the **Why**

Move to the Head
Explain the **How**
of What You Want Done
And Give Evidence.

End with the Hands
What Actions Need to be Taken
and by When?

Change is taking place in health care today at an incredible pace. Simon Sinek notes from his research that leaders who use leadership communication starting with why are more effective and gain the respect and buy-in of their staff.[4] This is advice worth taking.

STRUCTURING YOUR MESSAGES

Leaders should be strategic in their communication to ensure that their messages are received in the way they intended. This is easier said than done. You need to consider five key areas when you have a message that needs to be conveyed to others. These include:

1. **Who is your target audience?**
   Your communication will vary depending on your target audience and their styles of communication. The strategy you use to present information to staff could be different than how you will communicate with your executive team. Ask yourself what the target audience needs to know, how much background they already have on the issue, and their communication preferences.

2. **What is the message?**
   The message that you want to convey is an essential consideration in how you structure the communication. Is it intended to be strictly informational, or is action needed? If it is a crucial action item or policy change, communication needs to occur using multiple channels and be repeated across time.

3. **Is this message time-sensitive?**
   If the information is time-sensitive, you need to communicate it as soon as possible. Sometimes, new leaders delay communication, and their team learns about changes in policies or employee benefits from staff on other units. Staff loses trust in leaders when they are not transparent with time-sensitive information. Avoid communicating on weekends and holidays when possible.

4. **What is the impact on the target audience?**
   Leaders often underestimate the impact of the content of messages. You may think that your news involves a small change in current practice, but the staff may view it differently. If the content has a significant impact on the target audience, you need to think through the most effective way to deliver it strategically.

5. WHAT IS THE BEST METHOD FOR THIS COMMUNICATION?

When a message is likely to evoke strong emotions, communication is best-done face to face when possible so you can quickly clear up any misunderstandings. If the communication involves a complicated change in practice, email may not be the best initial approach.

Unlike face-to-face or phone communication, messages in email can be easily misinterpreted and escalate into major dramas. My experience with nurse leaders is that they often err in putting too much content into messages. The key points that they intend to make are not clear. It is better to adopt a *less is more* mindset when writing emails. The following are some dos and don'ts with email messages:

EMAIL DOS

- Have a clear subject and note if action is needed.
- Keep the email to three key points and bullet those points.
- If it is an action item – bold the date in the email.
- Think through what recipients need to receive the email.
- Keep it upbeat and positive.

EMAIL DON'TS

- Do not use email for an emotionally laden topic.
- Do not send it without careful proof-reading.
- Do not cc people who do not need to see the email.
- Do not use "reply to all" unless it is crucial.
- Do not ignore your email.

If an initial email is misunderstood or evokes strong emotions, pick up the phone. Clarification is much more challenging in email, and follow-up emails can make things worse. When you send emails, respond to comments and questions. When nurse leaders do not respond to their email or phone messages, it is frustrating for staff and colleagues. Sometimes, leaders do not respond to requests because they do not want to answer negatively, but in many respects, no answer is far worse than a negative reply. Your response time to email or phone messages is a non-verbal cue about your leadership behavior. Research shows that the longer you take to respond, the more negatively you are viewed as a leader.[5] How you deal with requests or messages says something fundamental about how reliable you are. And that translates into trust. Improving your email communication could enhance your leadership reputation in ways that you might not anticipate, so it is worth your time to incorporate these best practices.

Messaging Bad News

Everyone likes good news, but sometimes leaders are asked to deliver bad news to their staff. It is even harder when you do not agree with the message or decision you are communicating. The bad news could be a change in benefits, involve redeployment to another clinical area, or it could be a layoff. Delivering these messages in a way that is compassionate yet clear is not easy. Leaders often struggle with communicating difficult news, sometimes making things worse through poor messaging. Here are five tips from Amy Gallo, an expert, in this area:[6]

- **Strategize the messaging** – Be sure you are clear about all aspects of the decision before talking with your employees. Specifically, you need to know how the decision was made, who was consulted, what other possibilities were discussed, and the rationale behind the outcome.
- **Start with a direct, clear message** – Let the staff know that this is a final, nonnegotiable decision. Do not sugar coat a tough decision.

Messaging is not only about what you say but your non-verbal communication as well. Do not avoid eye contact or slump your shoulders.

- **Explain the "why" of the decision** – Talk about the rationale and process used in decision- making. Explain the steps taken to arrive at a decision and any critical findings during the process. If staff can see that the decision-making process was sound and fair – the decision is often easier to accept. Do not share with your team that you disagree with a decision – you can advocate with your leadership, but you need to support it once a decision is made.

- **Allow staff to vent but not to debate** – Once you present the decision, ask staff for their reaction. Part of your role as a leader is to be the shock absorber for your team. Do not debate the merits of the decision or feed into any criticism of the leadership.

- **Focus on the future** – Allow some time for the news to be absorbed and understood after the initial messaging. Some staff may want to speak with you privately about their concerns. Once that has happened – shift your focus to the future and moving forward. Do not have conversations that revisit the decision as this can be misunderstood by staff as opening the door for renegotiation.

Part of being a leader is being able to communicate in good times and bad. Winston Churchill was a firm believer in being very transparent with the British about how bad things were and could get during World War 2. He once said, *"The British nation is unique in this respect: They are the only people who like to be told how bad things are, who like to be told the worst."*[7] In some senses, I believe nurses are also like this. We are a profession that delivers and watches bad news delivered to patients every day. I found in my work that nurses often told me, *"Do not sugarcoat this – tell me how bad this could get,"*– and so I did.

LEADERS SPEAK IN AN AMPLIFIED VOICE

In many ways, leaders are like politicians when communicating. You are never off the record. New leaders often learn this the hard way. Roberto had gone to a strategic planning session with his executive leadership team. One of the strategies discussed to cut costs was the closure of low patient volume units. Roberto managed one of the units discussed for possible closure. During a staff meeting the following month, a nurse complained about staffing shortages on the unit. Roberto casually mentioned that it probably would be closed soon, and staffing cuts were the first step. The staff was shocked at this revelation. Roberto tried to calm them by saying that no final decision had been made, but the damage was done. Staff began to worry about the security of their jobs. His executive leadership team was upset with Roberto for talking about a plan that was in preliminary discussions.

As a leader, you speak with an amplified voice. Your messages carry weight. Your words matter. The words that we choose and how we deliver them does make a difference. If a leader is definitive in their language, advising staff with such terms as "your jobs are secure" or "you will be able to do this,"- you need to be prepared to deliver on these promises. Words used by leaders can either signal a high degree of optimism, inclusiveness, or teamwork or they can make a leader appear mistrustful and self-centered. Words can build up followers' self-esteem or cause pain, anger, frustration, and emotional withdrawal. Successful leaders understand the power of words and choose words to do the following:

1. **CREATE A CULTURE OF INCLUSIVENESS**

   The pronouns used by leaders can help build a culture of inclusiveness. Excessive use of the word *"they"* on a team is a sign of problems with harmony and teamwork. It also characterizes environments where there is a blame game going on. Instead of using the term *"they"*– leaders need to shift the language to the pronoun *"we."* The word *we* is one of the most important words in leadership language. It is inclusive, builds a team culture, and helps to break down silos in organizations. Never describe anyone as "*just a staff nurse.*"

2. Encourage Others

Words that are affirming help to make people feel good. Encouraging words help to get others through difficult times. Leaders need to work hard not to cut off the conversation with words like "*Yes - but* or, *Yes - however.*" These words indicate that you disapprove of what was said. When a team member introduces a new idea, a leader should avoid saying, "*I know that*" or "*I have done that before.*" Leaders who excessively use the word "*I*" instead of using the word "*we*" may be taking more credit than they deserve. Leaders also need to be careful about using the possessive pronoun "*my*" to describe "*my unit*" or "*my team.*" The word can imply a level of implicit ownership that others may resent.

3. Build Relationships

Building relationships with others is key to leadership success. Words that recognize the contributions and strengths of others help to create positive relationships. Every leader has probably had the experience of using just the right words in a relationship to help it grow or using the wrong choice of words that made the situation worse. Examples of words to avoid include: "What you *need* to do …", "What you *should* do," "What you *must* do," or "If I were you…. I *would.*" These are words that can completely shut down a conversation.

As your leadership journey continues, work hard to avoid making casual or inflammatory remarks. Leaders speak in an amplified voice and are judged by the words they use. Confucius said that "words are the voice of the heart." Learning to choose your words wisely will help you grow into the type of nurse leader your staff will not want to leave.

LISTENING – THE LEADERSHIP SUPERPOWER

When we talk about communication, we often forget about the importance of listening. Becoming a great listener can be your leadership superpower. To achieve this, you need to be more Yoda and less Superman. A Yoda restrains from jumping to conclusions and listens with curiosity. In conversations with staff, a Yoda tries to spend 80% of their time listening and only 20% of the time talking.

Listening is a skill that you can learn. Not listening is a habit and one you can break. A nurse leader shared with me what she does to stop her practice of breaking into conversations instead of letting others finish their thoughts. She has a sticky note on her computer that says WAIT. It stands for **W**hy **A**m **I** **T**alking? When she does this, she quiets her own agenda. The most effective leaders leave followers with the feeling that they are heard. Often, all staff wants to do is vent – not to have you jump in and give advice. This is where active listening becomes critical. The basic concept of active listening is repeating back to the nurse what you heard while maintaining eye contact.

No one expects you have all the answers. When leaders do not listen, staff may feel angry, disappointed, and disrespected. When leaders listen, their team is more engaged and, feels valued, respected, and more hopeful. Authentic dialogue does not happen when we pretend to listen and will not happen if we do not listen at all. You will improve your listening skills by learning to ask great questions such as those included in the leader toolkit in this book (Part 5). When you ask questions, you create a safe space for other people to tell you the truth. Leaders need this to be effective. We know that the best leaders are learners, and to learn well, we must listen well to learn something new.

KEY POINTS

✓ Communication is an essential leadership skill because of the impact excellent communication can have on productivity, quality, morale, and retention.

✓ Taking the time to understand the communication styles of your staff and other leaders will help you meet their needs more effectively.

✓ Leaders who use leadership communication from the inside out are more effective and gain the respect and buy-in of their staff.

✓ In many ways, being a leader is like being a politician; you are never off the record.

✓ Becoming a great listener can be your leadership superpower.

CHAPTER 7

GIVING EFFECTIVE FEEDBACK

G iving constructive feedback can be challenging, but it is essential to build a culture of continuous improvement. As a leader, you want your staff to view feedback as a positive tool to help them grow. Through feedback, we learn what we are doing right or what we may need to do differently. A culture of feedback begins with the leader and how you accept feedback given to you. Nurse leaders are in a unique position to role model how to ask for and receive feedback. All of us have blind spots. As a leader, you will not always behave, complete tasks, or interact with others in the way that you might intend. When the leader views feedback given to them as a gift and is not emotionally triggered by it, they set a powerful example for staff. When leaders demonstrate feedback-seeking behaviors, it results in higher job satisfaction for staff, greater creativity on the team, and lower turnover. As we discussed in Chapter 5, leaders can seek specific feedback by asking the following questions:

1. What should I *stop doing*?
2. What should I *keep doing*?
3. What should I *start doing*?

To establish a team culture of feedback, you want to promote a need for a growth mindset. Some staff members equate feedback with failure. You want to convey the message that constructive feedback, when used, can lead to significant improvements in performance. Dr. Carol Dweck is a pioneer in researching how adopting a growth mindset can transform how we view feedback.[8] Mindsets are the self-theories that people hold about themselves. Our mindset can either be fixed or growth oriented. Figure 5 illustrates how staff will perceive feedback differently depending on their mindset.

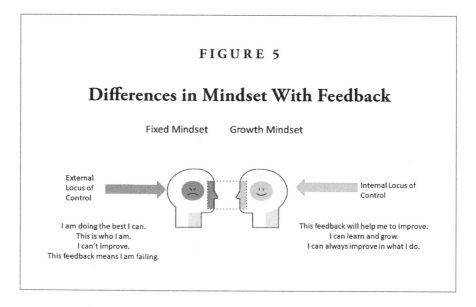

FIGURE 5

Differences in Mindset With Feedback

Fixed Mindset   Growth Mindset

External Locus of Control

Internal Locus of Control

I am doing the best I can.
This is who I am.
I can't improve.
This feedback means I am failing.

This feedback will help me to improve.
I can learn and grow.
I can always improve in what I do.

When staff is encouraged to have a growth mindset, negative feedback is more comfortable because they can fix their performance problems without becoming defensive. The key to helping staff move from a fixed mindset to a growth mindset is the approach you use in giving feedback. The following are five steps to improve how you provide formal feedback:[9]

1. **Prepare your feedback in advance** – Think about in advance the key messages you want to convey. Consider the method you will use (face to face, email). Have clear examples to illustrate the points you want to make. Be timely in how you deliver feedback after a critical incident.
2. **Create psychological safety** – Make it safe for the staff member by conveying that you have their best interest at heart. Be approachable and empathetic.
3. **Use concrete examples** – Gather concrete examples to illustrate points that you want to make. State which parts of the feedback are based on fact and which factors are your opinions.
4. **Listen** – Practice good listening skills. Allow the staff member time to absorb the feedback and respond to whether they see the event or situation in the same way you do. Ask if they have ever received this type of feedback before.
5. **Stay Future Focused** – Feedback should be solutions-oriented and future-focused. Coach the staff member on how they can use this feedback to improve their future performance.

When you recruit new team members, let them know that you are building a culture of feedback, and that they should expect professional feedback. Hayley, manager of a mother-baby unit, asked potential hires during the interview about specific feedback they had received about their professional performance either at their last job or school. She was also interested in how they had reflected on the input and what actions they took to improve. Through doing this, Hayley learned that some nurses could not identify in interviews any examples of when they had been given and used feedback. When she did hire a candidate, this initial discussion set the foundation to expect and use feedback. By doing this, Hayley demonstrated one of the seven habits of highly effective people – begin with the end in mind.[10]

Much of the feedback that nurse leaders give happens more informally. It may be suggestions that you provide during leader rounding. It could be observing a staff member struggling with an issue and sharing your advice or perspective. Generation Z and Millennial nurses want and expect more feedback than previous generations.[11] If they do not receive it, they are more likely to leave. Regular feedback from leaders is a powerful tool to develop your team and support their career growth.

The art of providing feedback is like a muscle that grows when used frequently by the leader. Becoming skilled in the art of both positive and negative feedback is crucial to being an effective leader. Like all skills, giving useful feedback takes practice and sometimes courage. When it is done well with the right intentions, feedback can lead to remarkable performance and mindset changes.

When Staff are Defensive

Some staff become defensive when you attempt to provide constructive feedback. Javier, a new manager in PACU, found himself in this situation with Shelly, one of his most experienced nurses. She ignored his suggestions and gave him the silent treatment when he tried to initiate feedback conversations with her. Javier acknowledged that she had excellent clinical skills, but there were areas where she could continue to improve like any professional. Understanding why people act defensively is essential to improving your approach to giving feedback in these difficult situations. The following are three questions to ask yourself when a staff member is defensive:

1. Are they only defensive with me, or do they also act this way with others?
2. Is this a long-standing behavior or a one-time incident?
3. Is this individual a perfectionist?

If the staff member is only defensive with you, they may not trust you or feel psychologically safe in your presence. They could think that you are overly critical of them. In some ways, this is the easiest of three problems to solve because you can change your behavior and build trust. When it is a long-standing behavior, a staff member may use defensiveness to control others and circumvent accountability. Leaders get worn down by defensiveness and often do not provide feedback to avoid confrontation. When you see this happening, it is crucial to confront the behavior.

Dealing with staff who are perfectionists can be the biggest challenge on the list above. Brene Brown has noted that shame is the birthplace of perfectionism.[12] Perfectionism is a mistaken belief that if we live a perfect life, act perfect, and look perfect, we can minimize the pain of blame, judgment, and shame. There is a strong association between professional performance and self-worth for the perfectionist. Any professional feedback may be perceived as criticism. Perfectionists often have an intense fear of failure. Nurses who are perfectionists need to feel very psychologically safe to accept input constructively. Upon reflection, Javier recognized that Shelly was a perfectionist. She had a high need for control and was quick to point out problems. Building trust with her would be crucial to her accepting feedback more constructively and reframing it, so it was not a threat to her self-worth.

GIVE DIFFICULT FEEDBACK

For most leaders, giving positive feedback is effortless, but negative feedback is more challenging. Leaders often choose to avoid discussions with staff, that they think will end in a confrontation. However, when problematic behavior is not addressed, it impacts the team's morale and erodes trust in the leader. Failure to address performance issues on your team can have serious ramifications.

Using an evidence-based framework for feedback conversations can help leaders stay on track with the feedback they want to deliver and avoid the drama that sometimes accompanies negative behavioral feedback. The Center for Creative Leadership has developed an SBI (situation-behavior-impact-way forward) model that is easy to remember and effective when used.[13]

Situation – The situation needs to be described along with the specific details of what happened and when. The feedback needs to be timely so that the staff member remembers the situation.

Behavior - The specific conduct that feedback is given about should be described fact-based and judgment-free.

Impact – The effect that the behavior had either positively or negatively is described.

Way Forward – Your expectations for the future and discussion about behaviors that may need to change. Some questions to ask as you discuss the way forward include the following: [14]

- What don't I know about this situation?
- How do you know your perceptions are accurate?
- What could you have done differently in this situation?
- How would you handle this situation differently in the future?
- How can we fix this?

LaTonya, director of an emergency department, used this approach with Renee during the COVID pandemic. Renee had excellent clinical skills, but she was extremely negative, escalating even minor situations into major dramas on the unit. Other staff found her difficult to work with. Renee was overly critical of the executive leadership team during COVID-19 – including LaTonya, her manager. LaTonya tried to be supportive, listening to her concerns both privately and in staff meetings.

The negativity spun out of control and impacted the morale of the ED staff. During a staff meeting, she described PPE policies as indicating how management must think nurses are dispensable. LaTonya recalls how she quickly followed up using the SBI approach with the following dialogue:

Situation - At our staff meeting this morning, we were discussing the new PPE policies.

Behavior - You said that our health system leaders must think nurses are dispensable.

Impact - It may not be your intent, but your negative comments impact the morale of the ED team when none of us have extra energy to deal with negativity.

Way Forward - I need your support and commitment to show up differently here at work. We need to discuss how you will demonstrate a more positive approach in the future.

HOLDING CRUCIAL CONVERSATIONS

Sometimes leaders avoid giving feedback, and the situation escalates to a crucial conversation. Whether they are about professional practice issues, time and leave problems, patient safety concerns, or disrespectful behavior, these conversations with staff are not easy. According to authors Patterson, Grenny, McMillian, and Switzler, a crucial conversation is one in which there are strong emotions, opposing opinions, and high stakes.[15] Learning to conduct these tough conversations effectively is a vital nursing leadership skill. Guidance for these conversations include the following:

1. **Start with the heart** - Before you begin a crucial conversation, ask yourself what you want to see as an outcome and what is at stake. Begin with the right motives. Do you want to help a staff member improve their performance or behavior? If the situation moved beyond this, do you need to help the staff member recognize the need to resign or seek a transfer to another area? Is there an error in judgment that you need to discuss with a staff member who always reacts defensively? Be clear about your goals before you hold the conversation to keep it on track, but recognize what is at stake here for you, the other individual, and your relationship.

2. **Learn to look** - The goal of a crucial conversation should be to maintain a dialogue. You want to avoid the conversation moving into a situation where both parties become defensive, and the discussion breaks down. When conversations feel safe, the dialogue will be free flowing. When it feels unsafe, the conversation can easily break down. Be a vigilant monitor of how you are behaving in a conversation and the impact you are having. Behave in a way that will help you to achieve the outcome you seek.

3. **Make it safe** - Make it safe for both you and the other party to have a challenging conversation. Sometimes, these conversations become contentious not because others dislike the conversation's content but because they believe you have malicious intent. Mutual purpose becomes essential in creating a zone of safety. Identify a shared goal. Look for points of agreement.

4. **Master your story** - When the crucial conversation involves something that has made you personally angry, it is important to get in touch with your feelings about the situation. Why do you feel the way you do and have strong emotions? What is the appropriate way to respond? Separate fact from the story by focusing on behavior.

5. **State your path and explore the path of others** - In an unemotional way, it is essential to share your facts and perspectives during a crucial conversation. At the same time, find out what

the other person is thinking. Look for areas of agreement and be sincere in your desire to listen to what is said. Ask questions to increase understanding.

6. **Move to Action** - To successfully conclude a crucial conversation, it is vital to reach a consensus about what will happen next. Document who will do what, by when, and decide on the plan for follow-up.

Crucial conversations are rarely easy to conduct, which is why we sometimes avoid them until situations spiral out of control. Do not allow yourself to get drawn into one of these conversations on the spur of the moment. The key to success in these conversations involves careful planning of your approach to the conversation, what you intend to say, and what you hope as an outcome. Writing down some key points can help keep you on track. Some seasoned nurse leaders use their colleagues as sounding boards to practice conducting conversations where they expect considerable pushback from the staff member involved. These crucial conversations about tough issues can be especially tricky for beginning nurse leaders and sometimes personally painful. Over time, leaders realize that these conversations are necessary, improve their relationships with others, and help them grow as leaders.

RECOGNITION IS A FORM OF FEEDBACK

All staff wants to be valued for their contributions and receive feedback about great work. As a leader, you can hardly give recognition often enough. Nurse leaders often get busy and forget to thank staff or express appreciation for a job well done. Some guidelines with recognition feedback include the following:

- Do not delay praise – so do it sooner rather than later.
- Do it because you are appreciative and be sincere.

- Be as specific as possible by providing details of what has led to the recognition.
- Make it personal – either in person or a hand-written note.
- Do not mix criticism and praise.

Individualization is the key when it comes to rewards and recognition. It is powerful when leaders provide recognition in a way that is meaningful to their employees. Some of your staff will want tangible awards or gifts. For others, a note of thanks or words of recognition will matter most. Some staff loves public recognition of their achievements while others would prefer to get it in a one-to-one conversation. It is impossible to provide individualized praise without asking staff questions about their preferences. Here is a set of items you can ask each of your direct reports, one-on-one:

- What contributions/successes do you want to be recognized for?
- When you accomplish something worthy of recognition, who do you want to know it?
- What is the best gesture of recognition you have ever received? Why was it the best?
- What form of recognition is most meaningful to you?

Look for opportunities to shine the light on your staff. When leaders fail to say thank you or take the recognition for themselves, staff feel devalued. Selena found this when she assumed leadership in a critical-care unit that had recently received the Beacon Award. Although the critical-care staff had worked hard to achieve the recognition, the previous director took the lion's share of the spotlight in publicity around the announcement. The team resented this. Selena realized that authentic leadership influence occurs by making others successful. She was determined moving forward to shift the recognition to staff by doing the following:

- Ensure that critical-care staff is nominated each year for the Daisy award.
- Recognize staff accomplishments at every staff meeting.
- Have staff present to receive and accept all future awards and recognition.
- Have staff deliver reports on unit outcomes to senior leadership.
- Find funding for critical-care staff to present at conferences on unit accomplishments.
- Introduce high-performing staff to others as "superstars."

Wise nurse leaders know that one of the most effective forms of employee acknowledgment and recognition occurs when a manager gives credit publicly where credit is due. The essence of leadership is to get work done through the efforts of others. Use recognition feedback to shine the light on staff and improve morale.

KEY POINTS

✓ As a leader, you want your staff to view feedback as a positive tool to help them grow.

✓ To establish a team culture of feedback, you want to promote a need for a growth mindset

✓ Understanding why people act defensively is essential to improving your approach to giving feedback in these difficult situations.

✓ Using an evidence-based framework like SBI for feedback conversations can help leaders stay on track with the feedback that they want to deliver.

✓ It is powerful when leaders provide recognition in a way that is meaningful to their employees.

CHAPTER 8

PROMOTING CONSTRUCTIVE CONFLICT

Today's healthcare workforce is composed of staff with different values, beliefs, and attitudes. These differences can and sometimes do lead to conflict. Conflict is central to all interactions because of the diversity of human experience. It will always be present on teams whenever there is a difference in opinion about something we care about or others' expectations that are different than ours. Some leaders see conflict as undesirable and fail to recognize that it can provide a source of growth and creativity. When your staff successfully manages conflict, it can lead to better decision-making, improvements in processes, and team cohesiveness.

When leaders avoid dealing with conflict, the conflict may escalate and interfere with the team's work. Unresolved disputes can lead to a loss of productivity and the turnover of valuable employees. Those involved in the conflict can pay a heavy price that impacts their health, leading to depression, anxiety, and sleep loss.[16] Patrick Lencioni, who is well known for his work on team dysfunction, has written about the importance of trust and conflict acceptance in creating environments that lead to the unfiltered and passionate debate of ideas. His research indicates that a team's inability to resolve conflict successfully is one of the five characteristics of dysfunctional teams.[17]

In healthcare settings, the biggest losers in unresolved conflict are often patients. Root cause analysis studies done by the Joint Commission on Accreditation of Healthcare Organizations indicate that a breakdown in communication among caregivers is a top contributor to sentinel events.[18] Often, these breakdowns in communication are a result of unresolved conflicts. The Joint Commission developed specific leadership standards addressing conflict resolution, noting that a significant barrier to conflict resolution in health care settings is a culture of avoidance among health professionals.

Seeing constructive conflict as an opportunity to improve is a paradigm shift for some nurse leaders who strive for team harmony and bury any discord. (Figure 6)

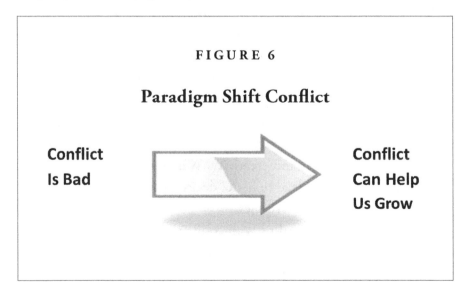

FIGURE 6

Paradigm Shift Conflict

Conflict Is Bad

Conflict Can Help Us Grow

DEVELOPING CONFLICT COMPETENCE

Conflict competency is your ability to use cognitive, emotional, and behavioral skills to increase the likelihood of a positive outcome while reducing the possibility of escalation or harm.[19] Self-awareness about your attitudes toward conflict is essential. If your paradigm is that conflict is destructive, you are less likely to engage in constructive conflict. Shifting your thought paradigm to believe that navigating conflict can lead to growth is vital to develop conflict competence.

Leaders also need to understand their emotional responses in conflict to regulate them effectively. If you find conflict stressful and anxiety-producing, you may avoid it or shut down in conflict situations. Some leaders become angry and feel threatened during disputes. They engage in verbal fights and competitive posturing. Understanding your conflict management style, hot buttons, and emotional triggers is essential to controlling them. You need to learn to cool down, slow down, and engage constructively.

Well-honed leader communication skills are crucial to becoming more competent with conflict management. Leaders who effectively manage conflict seek first to understand through careful listening before they share their perspectives. The goal is to work together. In conflict situations, communication can easily breakdown, so keeping the communication going is critical.

STYLES OF MANAGING CONFLICT

Not every leader manages conflict in the same way, nor should every conflict be handled using only one conflict management style. Although many of us can flex our style when needed, we usually have a preferred method of managing conflict, which is essential to identify. The most widely used assessment uses the styles outlined in the Thomas Kilmann

Conflict Resolution Model. There are five primary modes of managing conflict, depending on your assertiveness versus cooperativeness.[20] These five styles include: *avoiding, accommodating, competing, collaborating, and compromising.*

- **Competing** is an assertive and uncooperative approach to conflict. You pursue your concerns with little attention to the other›s interests. It is a power-oriented approach to a conflict where you defend your position and follow what you believe to be your rights. Your goal in conflict situations is to win.
- **Accommodating** is an unassertive and cooperative approach to managing conflict, which is the opposite of competing. You ignore your own needs to satisfy the concerns of the other party. Even though you may disagree, you will obey another person's order or yield to their point of view to keep the peace.
- **Avoiding** is both an unassertive and uncooperative response to conflict. When using an avoiding style, you do not engage in the conflict. You might intentionally choose to overlook a contentious issue, postpone a discussion, or withdraw entirely from the conflict situation.
- **Collaborating** is both an assertive and cooperative response that is the opposite of avoiding. You work with others to find a solution that fully satisfies their needs and concerns while meeting your own needs.
- **Compromising** is an approach where you moderate your level of assertiveness and cooperativeness. When compromising, you seek to find a mutually acceptable win-win solution for both individuals.

We should develop the capability to use all five modes of conflict-resolution depending on the type of conflict. Awareness about your preferred style is critical because it could be your default style, particularly in stressful situations. Studies indicate that many nurse leaders use avoidance as their primary response to conflict.[21] Nurse leaders whose preferred natural style is avoidance will need to push themselves to engage in conflict resolution, especially when it is contentious. In contrast, if a nurse leader is naturally overly competitive in style, they may have challenges reaching successful conflict resolution because their approach is too combative. The key is to identify the right approach for each unique situation to be both an effective mediator and coach staff to resolve a conflict.

MEDITATING CONFLICT

Leaders have three choices in conflict situations. The first is to do nothing. Doing nothing could be the right choice if you anticipate that the conflict will quickly resolve or is time limited. If a dispute is between two staff members, and one has already accepted a position on another unit, the leader may decide not to get involved. The second choice is to coach staff to mediate their conflict. Sometimes, conflicts can be settled by staff members without the leader intervening. If individuals have a good working relationship, this can be the right choice. It will also be a good decision if the situation involves a charge nurse who needs to develop conflict resolution skills in his or her role.

Ideally, you want to coach your team members to work through conflict situations, but this is not always possible. Your third choice is to become directly involved and mediate the conflict. Look for the following warning signs that indicate it is time to get involved:

1. There is a lack of respect.
2. A staff member has threatened to resign because of the conflict.
3. The conflict is impacting team morale or quality of care.

Angelina, a behavioral health team leader, made the decision to mediate a conflict. Two members of her team were in a long-standing conflict that began long before she assumed her leadership role. Whenever they were scheduled together on a shift, there was drama. They argued openly about assignments and refused to provide each other with the team backup needed to provide care. Before mediating the conflict, she sought to learn as much as possible about why it was happening. The two staff members were from different generational groups and had different beliefs. What began as minor disagreements had escalated over time. They lost respect for one another. Angelina knew that this conflict mediation would be challenging and recognized that it impacted care and morale. She planned the session using the following conflict resolution process recommended by experts: [16]

1. **Bring the individuals in conflict together to discuss the problem.** When there is a conflict between individuals, the leader must bring the parties together. There may be resistance to this from those involved in the conflict, but it is an essential first step. As a leader, you want to create psychological safety for those involved in the dispute. If everyone can tell their story without others involved in the conflict present, you risk polarizing their positions and eroding trust. Conflict resolution conversations should not be a one-sided monologue.

2. **Agree to ground rules for discussion that are acceptable to all parties.** When mediating a conflict, it is important to establish ground rules about behavior and language expected during the discussion. These ground rules could include no interrupting, no personal attacks, using the word "*I*" to specify personal reactions, and no discussion of issues unrelated to this specific conflict.

3. **Let the other person clarify his or her perspective and opinion on the issues.** Those involved in the conflict should share their perspective on the conflict and what outcomes they hope to achieve from the mediation. Open-ended questions to clarify

feelings are essential. If a staff member states that they feel disrespected, seek more information by asking what leads them to that conclusion. Applying a time limit to the discussion may be helpful. Doing so helps each person speak about the issues that matter and reduces conversational clutter with little bearing on the conflict. The goal is to shift from blaming to clarifying one's own needs in the dispute.

4. **Highlight some common ground that all involved can agree on.** Finding common ground in conflict is significant because it can serve as a reference point to help bring the discussion back on track. Most staff will agree with a mutual goal to provide the best possible patient care. When conflict escalates, you can get the individuals back to the point of common ground.

5. **Develop interventions collaboratively and agree to disagree on points of contention**. Presenting a conflict as a black-or-white, right-or-wrong situation heightens the tension. Work to help individuals develop interventions collaboratively. The conversation should be solutions-focused rather than dwelling on the problems. Where there is a point of significant contention, it may be necessary to agree to disagree.

6. **Summarize and identify the next steps.** The final step is to summarize what was said, identify the next steps, and any follow-up discussions that you may need to schedule. A positive outcome in most conflicts will be to open the lines of communication and re-establish working relationships. Leaders can help staff openly acknowledge the differences in attitudes, values, and beliefs that have led to the conflict and ways to be more respectful in the future.

Angelina carefully planned the mediation session with the two staff members. She developed some questions to ask both staff members during the session:

- *What part have you played in the conflict?*
- *How do you know your perspective is accurate?*
- *Have you tried looking at this from your coworkers perspective?*
- *What needs to be true that is not true today to resolve this conflict?*
- *What would a good outcome look like in this situation?*
- *How will we know that the conflict is over?*

Planning helped Angelina keep the conversation on track when emotions ran high. She set clear expectations that a failure to move toward more constructive conflict resolution was not an option. Angelina knew that this would not be a one-and-done conversation. She laid out a plan that would involve one-three and six-week follow-up discussions to assess progress. She remained optimistic in her approach, even though the conversations were energy draining.

POST-CONFLICT REFLECTION

Your overall goal in the mediation of conflict is to help the team members work more effectively together to address patients' needs. Navigating, through conflict, provides opportunities for both staff and nurse leader growth. We gain skill and confidence in constructively managing conflict by using every situation as a learning opportunity. Post-conflict reflection is a structured way to think about your lessons learned. Some interesting post-conflict questions to ask include:

- What went well during this conflict discussion?
- What would you do differently in the future?
- How did you grow from this situation?
- What did you learn from this situation that could prevent it from happening again?

The more you do it and reflect on what you would do differently the next time, the more effective you will be in promoting constructive conflict mediation.

KEY POINTS

✓ When your staff successfully manages conflict, it can lead to better decision-making, improvements in processes, and team cohesiveness.

✓ If your paradigm is that conflict is destructive, you are less likely to engage in constructive conflict.

✓ Not every leader manages conflict in the same way, nor should every conflict be handled using only one conflict management style.

✓ Understanding your conflict, hot buttons, and emotional triggers are essential to controlling them.

✓ Your overall goal in the mediation of conflict is to help the team members work more effectively together to address patients' needs.

CHAPTER 9

ENCOURAGING DIVERSE THINKING

I n the past decade, political, social, and cultural differences have led to increased polarization. Not surprisingly, an intolerance for different ideas has seeped into some work environments causing negativity, conflict, and incivility. In a 2015 New York Times op-ed, Christine Porath wisely reminded us that *"How we treat one another at work matters. Insensitive interactions have a way of whittling away at people's health, performance and souls."*[22] Creating work environments that embrace a diversity of thought is considered a new frontier in leadership.[23] The highest-performing teams are both cognitively and demographically diverse. Yet this diversity of ideas and viewpoints can be challenging to achieve on teams. There is a natural tendency to gravitate toward others who have the same beliefs that we do. Staff who think differently sometimes feel excluded by other team members. The following four elements need to be present to create more inclusive teams:

1. Staff feels that they are treated equitably and fairly by the leader with no favoritism.
2. Staff feels valued for what they bring to the team and a sense of belonging.
3. Staff feels psychologically safe to speak up without embarrassment, harassment, or retaliation.
4. Staff are empowered in their work and encouraged to develop by the leader.

Deloitte data indicates that the leader's behavior accounts for up to 70% of the tolerance for a diversity of ideas in an organizational culture.[23] To build environments that promote diverse thinking, nurse leaders need to do the following:

- Commit to diversity and inclusion as a core value in their leadership.
- Demonstrate the courage to embrace conflict and lack of harmony.
- Be aware of and monitor their own implicit biases and blind spots.
- Be open-minded and listen with curiosity to ideas that are different than your own.
- Be culturally intelligent, paying attention to the needs of others.
- Empower staff and build team cohesion.

Jack took a position as a neonatal ICU director and was surprised at how intolerant some staff were to others with diverse viewpoints. The culture was not one of inclusion. He was determined to encourage diverse thinking, as it was one of his core leadership values. During his onboarding, he learned that the previous leader had not promoted a culture of inclusion. Not all staff felt safe in expressing their viewpoints, nor did they believe they were fairly treated.

Jack formed a culture committee. The committee developed a new set of team values that included respect for different viewpoints. Jack pointed out to his team that you do not have to agree with others' views, but they are entitled to their opinions, and you should be willing to listen. He worked hard to role model the behavior. When Jack heard two staff loudly arguing about politics, he joined the conversation and coached them to reach a consensus on two agreement points. He understood the social drivers of human behavior and that finding common ground is the first step.

Jack dared to tackle this challenge even though it was not easy. He used his experience on his high school debate team to help him. Before debate forums, team members researched controversial contemporary issues. Ten minutes before debating, Jack would learn whether he was arguing for or against an issue. It was such a great exercise in critically thinking through both sides of any problem. He became used to having "strong opinions, weakly held." Jack uses these debate skills every day with staff. When there is a diversity of opinion - he always asks – "*What about this viewpoint could make it right?*" His team knows that he respects diversity in views. Jack encourages staff to speak up if they see things differently than he does. The staff knows that he is okay with a lack of harmony but not a lack of civility.

PSYCHOLOGICAL SAFETY

In rebuilding his culture, Jack understood the importance of psychological safety on the team. Dr. Amy Edmondson is an expert on psychological safety in the workplace. She provides the following description: "psychological safety describes the individuals' perceptions about the consequences of interpersonal risk in their work environment."[24] It consists of taken-for-granted beliefs about how others will respond when you put yourself on the line by asking a question, seeking feedback, reporting a mistake, or proposing a new idea. We weigh each potential action against a particular interpersonal climate, as in, "*If I do this here, will I be hurt, embarrassed or criticized?*" An act that might be unthinkable in one workgroup can be readily taken in another, due to different beliefs about probable interpersonal consequences."

Nurse leaders play a vital role in creating psychologically safe cultures for staff to question practices, report problems, or propose new ideas. Agreement or disagreement with the following statements are essential indicators of the level of psychological safety on a team: [24]

1. On this team, it is easy to speak up about what is on your mind.
2. If you make a mistake on this team, it is held against you.
3. People on your work team are usually comfortable talking about problems and disagreements.
4. People on this team are eager to share information about what does and does not work.
5. Keeping your cards close to your vest is the best way to get ahead on this team.

On a team where staff feels psychological safety, the staff has confidence that they will receive respect and consideration from others. A group with a culture of psychological safety encourages open discussion of challenging issues. It not only tolerates disagreement; it nurtures contrasting points of view. Leaders can help create these environments by developing and reinforcing the following team behaviors:

- **Show Civility** – Showing civility is the most important contribution people can make to creating and sustaining psychological safety. Attending to what others contribute and responding with consideration not only reduces anxiety but encourages creative thinking.
- **Argue with Respect** – Contrasting ideas are the most significant source of creativity. Team members need to learn to be tolerant of other viewpoints. Agreement on the team is not mandatory but agreeing to disagree respectfully should be.

- **Be supportive** – Using supportive language towards others should be an expectation. Humor does not excuse a put-down, nor does it make one palatable. People do not like it.

Feeling safe at work can increase a person's energy, enthusiasm, and zest for life. Nurse leaders who hold both themselves and the team accountable to behavioral standards that improve psychological safety can significantly impact creating a more positive and safe work environment.

VALUE GENERATIONAL DIFFERENCES

The band Buffalo Springfield recorded a popular song in the 1960s that began with the lyrics, *"There's something happening here. What it is ain't exactly clear."* It can feel that way to leaders when generational shifts occur in the workforce. Changes in workforce expectations often begin slowly. Nurse leaders sense changes but then the momentum seems to build. As you move through your leadership career, you may find at different points that some strategies that served you well at one point no longer work with the newest generation of nurses.[25]

Sarah, a perioperative nursing director experienced this in a leadership role across two decades. In her first decade of leadership, most OR staff members were either Baby Boomers (born 1946-1964) or Generation X (born 1965-1980). These nurses stayed in their roles for years with little staff turnover. Things began shifting in her second decade of leadership as Millennial nurses (born 1980-1996) joined her team. These younger staff members were more career-oriented, expressing a need to "get ahead." They wanted coaching and feedback. Many returned to graduate school to become nurse anesthetists or nurse practitioners. Turnover increased in the OR, and Sarah focused more of her attention on recruitment and retention. Baby Boomer nurses on her staff then began to retire in large numbers. Newer staff were Millennials, or Generation Z nurses (born 1997-2015) cohort. Work-life balance surfaced as a critical issue. The expectation of taking on-call coverage which had always been part of perioperative nursing now created dissatisfaction. Sarah was initially frustrated with how much flexing she needed to do in her leadership approach. Over time, she has come to appreciate these young nurses' qualities as they bring great ideas to the team.

These differences in the way different generations think about their work and life are not new. Thomas Jefferson once predicted that the United States would need a new constitution every 19 years to accommodate the differences in new generations' needs and thinking. Nothing should be unchangeable, he said, except the inherent and unalienable rights of man. Thomas Jefferson made these comments without knowing anything about generational theory. Interestingly, generational cohorts are designated by the year of their birth with periods between 17 and 22 years, remarkably close to the 19 years described by Jefferson. Generational theorists propose that generational cohorts are deeply influenced in their thinking by events, experiences, and technology that are part of their world during their formative years.

People who are born during a particular era share common experiences growing up. Their values and attitudes about work-related topics and life, in general, tend to be similar. A partial explanation of why this occurs is the shared experiences or defining moments that capture generational cohorts' attention and emotions during their formative years.[25]

Technology also plays a crucial role in influencing the thinking of generational cohorts. It is difficult to believe today, but most Baby Boomers did not have television as part of their early lives. Many Generation Z nurses had smartphones from a young age which became integral to how they learned, communicated, and socialized. It is understandable how difficult it might be for Generation Z nurses who check their phones up to 100x a day to leave them in their lockers to comply with hospital policies.[26] With their different attitudes, values, and preferred communication, new generations of nurses bring great strengths to the teams they join. Generations do think differently, and this diversity is good. Health care needs disruptive innovation. Innovation will only come with leaders who embrace diverse thinking about long-established practices and recognize that it prevents groupthink.

AVOID GROUPTHINK

Groupthink is a psychological phenomenon that occurs within a group of people when the desire for harmony or conformity results in an incorrect or flawed decision-making outcome. Group members try to minimize conflict and reach a consensus without critically evaluating alternative ideas or viewpoints. They may also isolate themselves from outside influences. In groupthink situations, loyalty to the group's way of thinking pressures individuals to avoid raising alternative solutions. When this occurs, there is a loss of individual creativity and independent thinking. There is no attempt to seek cognitive diversity when recruiting new team members.

John found this phenomenon when he joined a new health system as an urgent care center planner. John participated in a strategic planning session about potential locations for new centers. One of the sites proposed by the vice president for strategic planning was not ideal in John's assessment. There were others in the group who concurred with John's assessment. Their ideas were quickly overruled and not carefully considered in a groupthink situation. The decision turned out to be an expensive failure for the organization.

Nurse Leaders can prevent groupthink situations by coaching team members to appreciate diverse viewpoints. The following is advice from the experts:[27]

- Establish group norms to encourage and promote divergent thinking actively.
- Actively seek and value diversity on teams to include age, culture, education, and ideas.

- Ask whether there is a different perspective on issues discussed by the team.
- Reward truth speakers by acknowledging their contributions to the discussion.
- As the leader, do not voice an opinion until you have sought the opinion of team members.
- Embrace conflict – do not quell it in the interest of harmony.
- Before making a significant decision, go around the room and ask each member for the decision's pros and cons.

Some leaders see groupthink as being beneficial. When working with a large team, it can allow the group to make decisions, complete tasks, and finish projects quickly and efficiently. However, this phenomenon has costs and limits diverse thinking.

KEY POINTS

✓ Creating work environments that embrace a diversity of thought is considered a new frontier in leadership.

✓ Nurse leaders play a vital role in creating psychologically safe cultures for staff to question practices, report problems, or propose new ideas.

✓ Generations do think differently, and this diversity is good.

✓ Nurse Leaders can prevent groupthink situations by coaching team members to appreciate diverse viewpoints.

CHAPTER 10

DEVELOPING A COACHING MINDSET

What nurses expect from their leaders is changing. The nurse leader who operates using a command-and-control style will have challenges recruiting and retaining staff. Today's nurses want their leaders to be coaches who will help them learn and grow as professionals. In the recently published book, *It's the Manager,* Gallup researchers analyzed decades of survey data and found that the best managers are coaches.[11] They also discovered that both the Millennials and Generation Z want their leaders to be coaches, not bosses.

Coaching is a different approach to collaborating with and developing the potential of staff. When you coach, you provide staff with the opportunity to grow and gain expertise through more consistent feedback, counseling, and mentoring. The goal is to help others learn through self-exploration rather than teaching. When coaching, the relationship moves from being dominated by the leader to a partnership with staff. You do not wait until the annual review to discuss areas in need of improvement.

The effective leader coach takes the time to understand individual staff's motivations, enables optimal performance, and encourages professional success. Figure 7 illustrates the difference in how a traditional leader and leader coach communicates and collaborates with their staff.

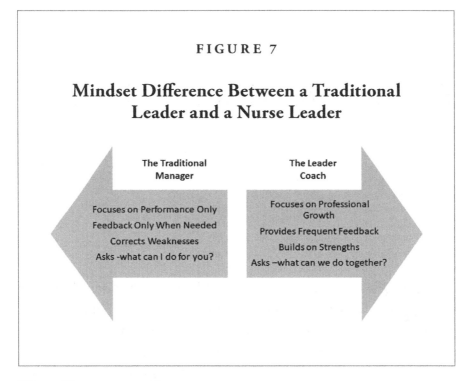

FIGURE 7

Mindset Difference Between a Traditional Leader and a Nurse Leader

The Traditional Manager

Focuses on Performance Only

Feedback Only When Needed

Corrects Weaknesses

Asks -what can I do for you?

The Leader Coach

Focuses on Professional Growth

Provides Frequent Feedback

Builds on Strengths

Asks –what can we do together?

KEY COACHING SKILLS

Effective coaching usually involves developing new skills and eliminating some bad habits. Most nurse leaders are promoted into a leadership role because of their excellent problem-solving skills in clinical practice. It is not surprising that managers see themselves as problem fixers because this is how they have added value in their roles. However, when you move into leadership, your success depends on others' success, and that requires coaching. To shift to becoming a leader coach, you need to resist the temptation to solve staff problems instead of developing their solutions.

There are five core coaching skills. They include the following:[28]

1. **Be fully present in conversations** with staff and avoid looking at communication devices.
2. **Practice active listening** and aim for talking only 20% of the time in coaching conversations.
3. **Ask open-ended questions** and recognize that the power of coaching is in the questions that you ask, such as: *What is on your mind?* – wait for a response and then ask -*And what else?*
4. **Practice direct communication** by helping staff identify self-limiting beliefs, their blind spots, or reframe their perspectives.
5. **Promote follow-up accountability** for goals set and maintain a feedback loop.

One of the most widely used coaching models is the four-stage GROW framework (Figure 8).[28]

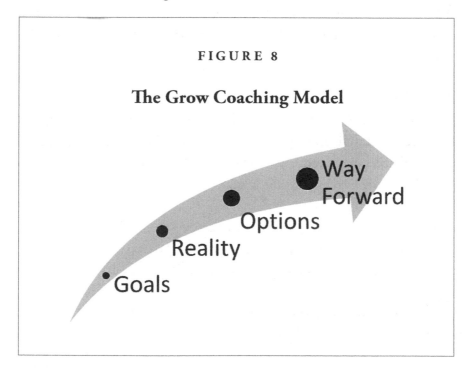

FIGURE 8

The Grow Coaching Model

There are many opportunities for coaching conversations in nursing. These include professional development, performance development, resilience, and career coaching.[29] Using the GROW model provides a structured way of conducting coaching conversations that can lead to better goal achievement.

Nate found this model was helpful in coaching his staff. He recently used it in a coaching session with Jake, a new graduate on his unit. Jake came to Nate after six months in his role and was looking for "a leadership role to move up the ladder." Nate was surprised because Jake was just beginning to gain clinical competence. He set up a coaching session. Nate thought through the conversation in advance. He felt Jake had good growth potential but was not ready yet to move into leadership. He did not want to kill his enthusiasm, but he needed to be realistic with him. Nate did believe that Jake could be ready to begin some emerging leadership classes in three to six months with some coaching. He used the GROW model to guide their conversation.

G - A goal is developed in partnership with the nurse. Nate and Jake reached the mutual goal of helping Jake reach clinical and other milestones to be ready to progress into leadership.

R - The current reality of this situation is discussed, including barriers and challenges. Nate discussed with Jake some of his current gaps in practice and the clinical competency milestones he needed to reach. He also explored how much Jake knew about the leadership role to ensure that this was the right path for Jake.

O - The options and pathways to achieve the goal. Jake and Nate agreed on some "grow in place" activities for Jake to begin to develop his leadership skills and complete his clinical competencies.

W - The way forward or plan with a timeline to achieve the goal. Jake and Nate established six months as the timeframe to complete the initial group of activities. They would meet once a month for follow-up coaching sessions.

BE MORE YODA LESS SUPERMAN

When you adopt a coaching mindset, you become much more Yoda and much less Superman.[30] Pilar struggled with this during her first year as a nurse manager. She wanted to support her nursing staff working on a busy medical-surgical unit. Many were new graduates in their first year of practice. Her door was always open, and nurses came in seeking her help. She would swoop in and fix the many problems and issues they had during their shift, receiving great feedback from staff about how responsive she was. Pilar fell behind in her administrative responsibilities and was quickly becoming burned out in the role. She finally sought help from her supervisor. He pointed out to Pilar that she needed to be less Superman and more Yoda.

Pilar recognized that her director was right. She was not empowering the nursing staff with the approach she was using. She had become an advice monster. The critical thinking skills of her team were not growing when she provided all the answers. She changed her leadership approach explaining to the staff that she would now begin coaching them to discover their own solutions to their challenges. Reflecting on her experiences, she realized that the new nurses often knew the right thing to do but lacked confidence in their decision-making. She encouraged them to think of one to two possible solutions to problems before they came to seek her guidance. Pilar began to ask the following questions when coaching new graduates:

- What solutions are you considering?
- What is the next action you will take in this situation?
- What evidence are you using to reach that conclusion?

- How do you know your assumptions are accurate here?
- How will you know if the patient's condition is improving?

Hardwiring the Coaching Habit

Given the demands of their leadership role and their span of control, nurse leaders may feel that they do not have the time to coach. If you reframe your thinking about the importance of coaching from a "nice to do" to a "must do," time will not be a problem. In today's job market, there is fierce competition for experienced nurses. If you commit yourself to be a leader coach, you could considerably decrease your time recruiting new staff and overall labor costs to your organization. Each percent change in RN turnover can save or cost a hospital an additional average of $306,400 per year.[31]

Any new change in our behavior changes work habits, and that can be challenging until it becomes routine. Coaching thought leader, Michael Bungay Stanier, has noted that this stuff sounds simple, but it is not easy.[32] The best way to start is to look for ways to embed quick-connect and check-in coaching conversations with staff into your current leadership activities such as team huddles, leadership rounding, or staff meetings. Commit to doing at least four brief coaching discussions with staff each day. These conversations do not need to be lengthy, but they do need to be authentic. Choose a few go-to questions that are comfortable for you to open the discussion with staff. Examples of good kickstarter coaching questions include:

- What is on your mind?
- What matters most to you in your work?
- What talents and skills do you have that you would like to use more often?
- What aspects of your work do you think you excel at?

- What do you want in your career?
- What support do you need to achieve your goals?
- What needs to be true that is not true today for you to achieve that goal?

There is strong evidence today that adopting a coaching mindset as a nurse leader has a significant impact on staff performance. Gallup recommends that if organizations prioritize only one leadership action to improve performance, they should equip their managers to be coaches.[10] Coaching is a skill set that can be learned, but it takes practice and intentionality. When leaders commit to coach, they can achieve a return on their investment of time through nurse retention, improved staff engagement, creation of healthier work environments, and better patient outcomes.

Key Points

- ✓ When you coach, you provide staff with the opportunity to grow and gain expertise through more consistent feedback, counseling, and mentoring.
- ✓ To shift to becoming a leader coach, you need to resist the temptation to solve staff problems instead of developing their solutions.
- ✓ When you adopt a coaching mindset, you become much more Yoda and much less Superman.
- ✓ The best way to start is to look for ways to embed quick-connect and check-in coaching conversations with staff into your current leadership activities such as team huddles, leadership rounding, or staff meetings.

PART 2 REFERENCES

1. Tutorials Point. The Rule of 7. Available at https://www.tutorialspoint. com/management_concepts/the_rule_of_seven.htm
2. Alessandro T., O'Connor M. *The Platinum Rule: Discover the Four Basic Business Personalities and How They Can Lead You to Success.* New York: Warner Books; 1998.
3. Communication Styles Inventory. Available at https:// health.ucdavis.edu/cppn/documents/classes/preceptor/ FinalCommunicationsStyleInventory.pdf
4. Sinek S. *Start with Why: How Great Leaders Inspire Everyone to Take Action.* New York: Portfolio Books; 2011.
5. Hefferman, M. (May 20, 2013 CBS Money Watch Blog). How do leaders respond to email? Available at https://www.cbsnews.com/ news/how-do-leaders-respond-to-email/
6. Gallo A. (March 30, 2015 HBR Blog) How to Deliver Bad News to Your Employees. Available at https://hbr.org/2015/03/how-t o-deliver-bad-news-to-your-employees.
7. Winston Churchill Quote. Available at https://www.brainyquote. com/quotes/winston_churchill_161175

8. Dweck CS. Mindset: *The New Psychology of Success.* New York: Penguin Publishers; 2016.

9. Roberts GL. Giving and receiving feedback. Available at LinkedIn Learning https://www.linkedin.com/learning/me

10. Covey SR. *The 7 Habits of Highly Effective People 30ᵗʰ Anniversary Edition.* New York: Simon & Schuster; 2020.

11. Clifton J, Harter J. *It's the Manager.* New York: Gallup Press; 2019.

12. Brown B. *The Gifts of Imperfection: Let Go of Who You Think You're Supposed to Be and Embrace Who You Are.* Danver MA:Hazelden Publishers; 2010.

13. Gentry WA. *Be the Boss Everyone Wants to Work For: A Guide for New Leaders.* Oakland CA: Berrett-Koehler; 2016.

14. Blatchley A. A nurse manager's guide to giving effective feedback. *Nurse Leader.* 2017,15(5), 331-334.

15. Patterson K, Grenny J, McMillan R, Switzler A. *Crucial Conversations: Tools for Talking When Stakes are High.* Second Edition. New York: McGraw-Hill; 2011.

16. May A. *Mediation and conflict resolution.* Allen May; 2018.

17. Lencioni PM. *The Five Dysfunctions of a Team: A Leadership Fable.* Hoboken, NJ: John Wiley & Sons; 2002.

18. Joint Commission. (2019, February 5). Most commonly reviewed sentinel event types. Available at https://www.jointcommission.org/assets/1/6/Event_type_4Q_2018.pdf

19. Runde C., Flanagan TA. *Developing Your Conflict Competence: A Hands-On Guide for Leaders, Managers, Facilitators and Teams.* San Francisco: Jossey-Bass; 2010.

20. Thomas KW., Kilmann RH. (2017). An overview of the Thomas-Kilmann Instrument. Available at http://www.kilmanndiagnostics.com/overview-thomas-kilmann-conflict mode-instrument-tki

21. Johansen M L., Cadmus E. Conflict management style, supportive work environments and the experience of work stress in emergency nurses. *Journal of Nursing Management, 24*(2), 211-218; 2015.

22. Porath C.(June 21, 2015 New York Times Op Ed). *How we treat each other at work matters.* https://www.nytimes.com/2015/06/21/opinion/sunday/is-your-boss-mean.html

23. Bourke J, Dillon B. (Deloitte Review - January 2018). The diversity and inclusion revolution: Eight powerful truths. Available at https://www2.deloitte.com/us/en/insights/deloitte-review/issue-22/diversity-and-inclusion-at-work-eight-powerful-truths.html

24. Edmonson A. *The Fearless Organization: Creating Psychological Safety in the Workplace for Learning, Innovation and Growth.* New York: Wiley; 2018.

25. Tulgan, B. (2020). The great generational shift. Available at https://rainmakerthinking.com/white-paper/the-great-generational-shift

26. Twenge JM. *IGen: Why today's super-connected kids are growing up less rebellious, more tolerant, less happy and completely unprepared for adulthood.* New York: Atria; 2017.

27. Booker C. *Groupthink: A Study in Self-Delusion.* Bloomsburg Continuum; 2020.

28. Whitmore J. *Coaching for Performance: The Principles and Practice of Coaching and Leadership.* London, England: Hachette UK; 2017.

29. Sherman RO. *The Nurse Leader Coach: Become the Boss No One Wants to Leave.* Rose O. Sherman; 2019.

30. Raymond J. *Good Authority: How to Become the Leader Your Team Is Waiting for.* Idea Press Publishing; 2018.

31. NSI Nursing Solutions (2020). National Healthcare Retention & RN Staffing Report. Available at https://www.nsinursingsolutions.com/Documents/Library/NSI_National_Health_Care_Retention_Report.pdf

32. Stanier MB. *The Coaching Habit: Say Less, Ask More & Change the Way You Lead Forever.* Box of Crayons Press; 2016

PART 3

LEADING HIGH-PERFORMANCE TEAMS

"Talent wins games, but teamwork and intelligence win championships."

MICHAEL JORDAN

CHAPTER 11

BUILDING COHESIVE TEAMS

Most of us, at some point in our careers, have worked on a great team. These are unforgettable experiences where we feel that we are at our best, and anything is possible. Yet, these high-performance work teams rarely happen naturally. Teams need to be built and coached. Guiding team members to communicate, navigate conflicts, and effectively work together is challenging. In healthcare, teamwork is even more essential because the stakes are higher. Team synergy and interdependence are vital for quality patient outcomes.

Work teams today are more diverse in every way. In many nursing settings, team members do not work together consistently. The composition of team members can change on a shift-by-shift basis. Nurse leaders are often highly dependent on charge nurses or clinical managers to lead the team effectively at the frontlines of care. Selecting and retaining team members can be difficult in this competitive labor market. There are shortages of experienced nurses in almost every clinical specialty.

Focusing on building a cohesive team has never been a more critical priority for nurse leaders.

We know great teamwork when we see it. The best teams do the following:[1]

- Have a common purpose that they work to achieve.
- Communicate openly and clearly.
- Have trust among team members.
- Respect the role and contributions of every team member.
- Provide team back up to one another when needed.
- Make it safe to ask questions and make mistakes.
- Appreciate the value of diversity and successfully navigate conflict.
- See their work as having an impact.
- Recognize that different team members have different work styles on teams, and each is important.

Communication breakdowns and conflict are inevitable on teams. The most common behaviors that create obstacles to effective teamwork include blaming others, turf protection, mistrust, and an inability to confront issues directly.[2] In the absence of complete trust, people are more likely to withhold their ideas, observations, and questions. Professionals are also more likely to leave teams that have trust issues. It is not surprising that ineffective teamwork is now recognized as a potential patient safety issue in our health care system. Team relationships live within the context of conversations that teams have or do not have with one another. When open and frank communication is not present, things can and do go wrong on teams.

RECRUITING NEW TEAM MEMBERS

To achieve effective teamwork, selecting, and retaining the right team members has never mattered more. Nurse leaders are the chief recruitment and retention officers for their units or departments. The evidence indicates that while nurses choose employment in organizations for what they have to offer, their reasons for leaving are usually challenges with their leader. We know from workforce research that the relationship with one's immediate supervisor plays a critical role in satisfaction and retention.[3] This relationship begins with the recruitment of new staff.

It is essential to be intentional in how you conduct interviews and review the qualifications of potential staff. Standardize your process to avoid leaving out any critical steps. The following is a sample interview checklist of best practices:

- ✓ Review the resume and application thoroughly before the interview.
- ✓ Evaluate any unexplained gaps in employment.
- ✓ Meet the candidate in the lobby and walk him/her to the unit.
- ✓ Begin the interview by asking why the candidate is applying for the position.
- ✓ Ask the same performance-based questions of each nurse candidate.
- ✓ Determine the candidate's expectations of you as their leader.
- ✓ Discuss with the candidate their career goals and professional development needs.
- ✓ Allow the candidate time to ask their questions.
- ✓ Assess how much due diligence the candidate has done in advance about the organization.
- ✓ Give the candidate a tour of the unit and an opportunity to meet the staff.
- ✓ Arrange peer interviews with the candidate if that is part of your selection process.
- ✓ Describe the follow-up selection process and provide the candidate with your business card.
- ✓ Develop a welcome letter to the unit and include a new hire packet with the job description, the organizational mission, vision, values, and other essential information.

There are many things that you need to consider as you hire new staff to join your team. One of the challenges in many healthcare environments today is the gap between high patient acuity and experienced staff availability. Ideally, you would strive for at least 50% or more of your staff to have both expertise and competency in your specialty area. This staffing mix is necessary to provide a thorough onboarding and orientation experience. You will want to consider all the following factors carefully:

- Education, work history, and experience.
- Current knowledge, skills, and abilities relative to the needs of the unit.
- Cultural fit with the mission, vision, and values of the organization and team.
- Current staff competency skill mix.
- Unit diversity goals
- Interpersonal skills and questions asked.
- Professionalism, enthusiasm, passion for the work.
- Patient advocacy and customer service.

PERFORMANCE-BASED INTERVIEWING

Performance-based or behavioral interviewing is an evidence-based method of interviewing staff. It involves giving candidates scenarios to assess their skills and includes open-ended questions about how they have managed specific previous job situations.[4] These answers provide insight into what you can expect in the future. Develop questions that assess the nurse's critical thinking using the position's critical anticipated competencies. Ask two to three questions for each competency and evaluate candidates on a sliding scale (1 – a skill not evident to 4 – strong evidence of skill) based on their responses. Examples of performance-based questions would include:

- Describe a situation in which you had to use your communication skills to de-escalate a problem with an angry patient. How did you manage the communication? How did you determine whether you were able to provide service recovery?
- Describe a time when you took personal accountability for a conflict and initiated contact with the individual(s) involved to explain your actions. What steps did you take? What was the result?
- Share a time when you received constructive feedback about something in your performance that needed improvement. What was it? What type of follow-up action did you take?
- You have just received your assignment of five patients from the charge nurse. Please walk me through how you would establish your priorities for the next hour.
- Please share an example of an important personal goal that you set and explain how you accomplished it.

Remember that interviewing is a two-way street so invite questions. As a manager, you should meet every candidate and ask about their expectations of you as their leader. Nurse leaders should never delegate the whole recruitment process to other members of their team. It sends a strong negative message to candidates about leader support and future interaction.

ONBOARDING NEW STAFF

The successful hiring of great candidates is only the first step. Staff retention begins with smooth onboarding. Dissatisfaction with employment often starts when new staff feels like they received a poor unit orientation. You should schedule a check-in at the end of the first week. Examples of questions to ask during a check-in include the following:

1. Has our team made you feel welcome?

2. Did you receive what you needed to begin work? (ex. new employee benefits information, ID badge, keys, email, and electronic medical record access)
3. Do you have questions that we have not answered?
4. What challenges do you see in your new role?
5. Is there anything we should change to help new staff better adjust to the unit?

Nurse managers often delegate these responsibilities to preceptors or unit educators, sometimes without good follow-up. Kristen made this mistake. She entrusted staff orientation to a unit-based educator. She assumed things were going smoothly and did no follow-up with new staff. New graduates received a thorough orientation as part of their residency, but the transition for more experienced nurses was hit and miss, depending on the unit workload. Kristen received several resignations from nurses within three months of their start dates. On exit interviews, she learned that some experienced staff felt they had a minimal orientation to the unit. Unfortunately, the damage was done, and none would reconsider staying on the team. Kristen changed her approach and established the following goals:

- **Be more intentional about welcoming new staff as a valued addition to the unit.** When new staff joins your community, they have no history. They may not be aware of important cultural norms, values, and behaviors. Leaders should ensure they are welcomed and introduced to others as a valued team member. Preceptors play a crucial role in the onboarding of new staff and should be carefully selected.
- **Ensure new staff has a thorough orientation, even if they have experience.** New staff should receive orientation at both the hospital and unit level. Review key policies and procedures. Use an orientation checklist to standardize the orientation. Do not skip

steps even when you are short-staffed. Always remember, you are setting the stage during orientation for a smooth transition.

- **Do regular check-ins on the progress of new staff members.** Nurse leaders should schedule a meeting with new staff at the end of the first week, at the 30 day point, at 60 days and mid-year to see how things are progressing and assess employment satisfaction.
- **Begin the professional development coaching process.** The late Dr. Stephen Covey recommended that we begin with the end in mind. Although performance coaching is critical during new employee transition, the staff member's long-term commitment will happen if you include professional development coaching. Learn about each new staff member's personal goals for their career and begin the individual development plan—help new staff develop at least two to three personal development goals. The goals should include actions and a timeline. Every manager should have a list of professional growth opportunities available for staff to "grow in place" on the unit, such as the following:
  - Certification preparation classes
  - Cross-departmental committee participation
  - New graduate mentor programs
  - Charge nurse classes
  - Unit practice council participation
  - Community leadership activities (heart walk, United Way drive, mission trips)

INTEGRATION INTO THE TEAM

Nurse leaders expect new staff to join their team and absorb the other team members' values, behaviors, and beliefs. Integration into a team is not that easy. Individual performance on teams is influenced by many things, including our generational cohort, culture, sex, assumptions, and work style. Individual workstyle on teams receives little attention in nursing, but it is an essential teamwork component. Kim Christfort and Suzanne Vickberg are two experts in team science. Their research on team chemistry reveals that most of us adopt one of four distinctive team member styles, as shown in Figure 9.[5]

FIGURE 9

Four Key Team Member Work Styles

PIONEER	DRIVERS
• VALUE POSSIBILITIES • WILLING TO TAKE RISKS • BIG PICTURE THINKERS • LOVE BOLD IDEAS AND CREATIVE APPROACHES	• VALUE CHALLENGE & MOMENTUM • WANT RESULTS • TACKLE PROBLEMS HEAD ON – OFTEN USING BLACK/WHITE THINKING • LIKE LOGIC AND DATA
GUARDIANS	**INTEGRATORS**
• VALUE STABILITY + HISTORY • WANT ORDER AND RIGOR TO DECISIONS • WANT DATA AND FACTS	• VALUE CONNECTION & RELATIONSHIPS • WORK TO GAIN CONSENSUS • DIPLOMACY IS IMPORTANT

Teams can struggle with a lack of trust or team backup when there is a failure to recognize different work styles. Nurses who have a pioneering style may have challenges understanding why those with a guardian style of working process change more slowly. Nurses who have an integrator style of working on teams may not understand a driver who focuses on completing the task at hand, sometimes forgetting about relationships. To build psychological safety on a team, as discussed in Chapter 9, both the leader and team members must understand each work style's key motivations.

PROMOTE INTERPROFESSIONAL TEAMWORK

Healthcare has been described as a team sport because the contributions of each discipline are so interdependent. Quality healthcare outcomes only happen in environments where there is strong interprofessional teamwork. Yet having a team of experts does not necessarily mean that you have an expert team. Getting interprofessional teams on the same page or even together in the same place to communicate can be challenging. The stakes are high if this does not happen. Most medical errors involve breakdowns in communication among team members. Ineffective interprofessional teamwork is a patient safety issue, and some experts believe it is strongly correlated to higher patient mortality.

Involvement and participation in patient care decisions are the keys to effective group functioning. Interprofessional teamwork requires individual involvement. Professionals cannot be allowed to opt-out because, given the opportunity, some will. Natalie had this experience on her surgical unit. She began an evidence-based best practice of interprofessional team rounding to improve patient experience and communication. Families and patients expressed appreciation for the opportunity to have all the team members together to discuss care. Then without notice or discussion, Natalie was told to discontinue the rounds. Key surgeon team members complained to the CEO that the patient rounds interrupted their workflow.

In thinking about why rounding had not worked, Natalie realized that she had not established a sense of urgency for the initiative. She realized that every discipline has a unique culture, language, and mental models involving patient care. For the surgeons on her team, surgical volumes and good patient outcomes were vital. The urgency of rounding needed to be directly linked to identification of quality and safety issues. We sometimes incorrectly assume that professionals will see the value in interdisciplinary teamwork. In their training, providers tend to become socialized into their professions and subsequently develop negative biases and naïve perceptions of other members of the health care team's roles.

As Natalie learned, the promotion of successful interprofessional teamwork meant changing current mental models. Nurse leaders often need to help other professionals see the value of collective knowledge and viewpoints on patient situations when planning care. A common issue in interprofessional teamwork is the problem of "turf battles." These struggles often involve issues of autonomy, accountability, and identity. Team members may be reluctant to take advice or suggestions from members of other disciplines.

To be effective, each member must have confidence that other team members can meet their responsibilities. There may be legal liability concerns for one's practice or losing control over one-to-one relationships with patients. An important reality is that the current reimbursement structure does not reward interprofessional teamwork activities. Time spent in an interdisciplinary meeting is not billable. If there are not strong interprofessional working relationships among executive team members, these behaviors may not be modeled or valued, as Natalie learned.

INTERPROFESSIONAL TEAM EFFECTIVENESS

Interprofessional teamwork requires the ongoing support of leaders who recognize that it is a massive cultural shift. Achieving a high level of interprofessional teamwork effectiveness does not come without challenges. When open and frank communication is not present, things can and do go wrong on teams. Some key questions to determine current interprofessional team effectiveness include the following:[6]

1. Do team members say "my patient" or "our patient"?
2. Do team members clearly understand the "scope of practice" and each discipline's key responsibilities on the team?

3. Do team members know each other's names, and how do they address each other?
4. Are team members respectful of other viewpoints and expertise?
5. Do team members ever round on patients together?
6. Do team members feel accountable to attend team meetings or care coordination conferences?
7. Are clear team goals established and roles assigned?
8. Can patients identify who the members of their care team are?
9. How does the team manage conflict or disagreement about care decisions?

The Interprofessional Education Collaborative (IPEC) has developed competencies for interprofessional practice that can guide team development. These competencies are in four domains: values/ethics for interprofessional practice, roles/responsibilities, interprofessional communication and teams, and teamwork.[6]

- **Values/Ethic Domain Expectations** - Work with individuals of other professions to maintain a climate of mutual respect and shared values.
- **Roles/Responsibilities Domain Expectations** - Use the knowledge of one's role and those of other professions to assess and address patients' health care needs appropriately and promote and advance populations' health.
- **Interprofessional Communication Domain Expectations** - Communicate with patients, families, communities, and professionals in health and other fields responsively and responsibly in a way that supports a team approach to promoting and maintaining health and preventing and treating disease.
- **Teams and Teamwork Expectations** - Apply relationship-building values and team dynamics principles to perform effectively in different team roles.

The above competencies have been integrated into academic programs. Medical students, nursing students, pharmacy, social work, and other related disciplines are taught together to learn how to communicate, work in teams, and discuss pertinent issues and trends such as ethics and policy. These same principles can and should be used in any healthcare environment to build strong collaborative interprofessional teams.

KEY POINTS

✓ Guiding team members to communicate, navigate conflicts, and effectively work together is challenging.
✓ Selecting and then retaining the right team members is key to effective teamwork.
✓ Individual workstyle on teams receives little attention in nursing, but it is an essential teamwork component.
✓ Interprofessional teamwork takes practice and the ongoing support of leaders who recognize that it is a massive cultural shift.

CHAPTER 12

CREATING A CULTURE OF QUALITY AND SAFETY

Value-based care is a key driver of reimbursement in today's healthcare system. Excellent patient outcomes that are high value occur in cultures where there is a relentless focus on safety and quality. Team culture has a significant impact on a wide range of metrics that are now key in healthcare environments and drive payment. Researchers who study disruptive behaviors on teams find direct linkages between teamwork and patient safety. Team members in dysfunctional cultures are much less likely to communicate about problems, resulting in more hidden medical errors. General David Morrison wisely reminded us that *"the standard we walk by is the standard we accept."*[7] Nurse leaders play a crucial role in identifying and correcting quality and safety issues.

Unfortunately, not all healthcare teams have a robust culture of quality and safety. Sometimes nurse leaders accept a leadership role and later find that their new unit has a toxic culture. This happened to

Linda, who took a director role in critical care in a large Magnet designated hospital. The last thing she expected to find was incivility and bullying on her new team. The one-to-one meetings that she held with staff during her first 100 days painted a disturbing picture of disruptive behaviors normalized in the culture. Linda knew from the work of Joe Tye and Bob Dent that team culture is the invisible architecture of a unit and has an enormous impact on quality outcomes.[8] She developed a plan to rebuild the culture using the following steps:

1. ASK FOR TEAM MEMBER FEEDBACK

Linda's one to one meetings with the staff provided her with a considerable amount of anecdotal data about what was happening on the team.

2. CONDUCT A TEAM ASSESSMENT

Linda received permission to use a disruptive behavior scale recommended by the Joint Commission.[9] The DB scales measure the presence of six evidence-based disruptive behaviors that are linked to ineffective teamwork, challenges with patient safety, and burnout. She found that 95% of staff reported two or more of the six disruptive behaviors.

3. FORM A UNIT CULTURE COMMITTEE

Linda knew she would need staff champions to help rebuild the culture. Six critical care nurses volunteered to be on the culture committee.

4. DEVELOP A TEAM VALUES STATEMENT

Linda understood a need to establish team core values that would discourage these behaviors in the future. The culture committee worked on this project with input from the staff. A no-bullying culture was one of the new core values.

5. HOLD TEAM MEMBERS ACCOUNTABLE

Linda understood that the team would need coaching around the new expectations. She would need to be vigilant in holding staff accountable, taking quick action when needed. A failure to do this can quickly lead to normalizing the type of deviant behavior she observed during her transition.

BULLYING ON TEAMS

As a nurse leader, your challenge is to identify staff bullying behaviors to stop the cycle. Renee Thompson, an expert on bullying in nursing, identified three key components to bullying:[10]

1. **A target** – The bully chooses a target, which can be a nurse or group of nurses such as new graduates on the unit.
2. **Harmful behavior** – The bully intends to inflict harm through criticism, sabotage, or setting a nurse up for failure. Intent to harm is the difference between constructive feedback and bullying.
3. **Repeated behavior** – The harmful behavior must be repeated over time.

Nurse leaders have a responsibility to analyze units' culture as Linda did and then watch closely for verbal and nonverbal cues in staff behavior. Some common cues include:

- Talking behind one's back instead of directly resolving conflicts.
- Making belittling comments or criticizing colleagues in front of others.
- Not sharing important information with a colleague.
- Isolating or freezing out a colleague from group activities.
- Making snide or abrupt remarks.

- Refusing to be available when a colleague needs assistance.
- Committing acts of sabotage that deliberately set victims up for a negative situation.
- Raising eyebrows or making faces in response to the comments of colleagues.
- Failing to respect the privacy of colleagues.
- Breaking confidences.

BREAKING THE CYCLE

A culture of zero-tolerance for bullying is the most effective leadership strategy to prevent its occurrence. Staff needs education about the behaviors that constitute bullying to help break the silence. Raising the issue at a staff meeting and letting staff tell their stories is a key step in rebuilding a culture. Staff needs to know that you will quickly be responsive when you observe bullying behavior, or when it is brought to your attention. Leaders need to engage in self-awareness activities to ensure that their leadership style does not support horizontal violence and bullying. The selection of preceptors who support a zero-tolerance policy is critical to orienting new staff about behavioral expectations. If your unit hires new graduates, provide staff opportunities to talk about their first year in practice and use these stories as powerful reminders to nurture our young. Breaking the cycle of bullying on a unit promotes better patient safety and can help both re-energize the staff with enthusiasm for their profession and create a healthier work environment.

EVIDENCE-BASED TEAM COMMUNICATION

Communication in healthcare environments can be challenging. Most quality and safety issues on healthcare teams occur because of communication problems. Clarity in communication is critical. Fortunately, there are good tools available to help communicate more effectively, and even more important, to make certain the communication is understood. Strategies and Tools to Enhance Performance and Patient Safety (TeamSTEPPS) is an evidence-based communication model developed for clinical practice with funding from the Agency for Healthcare Research and Quality.[11] These tools were developed for clinicians to communicate more effectively and build safer patient care environments. Tools in the model include SBAR, the Two-Challenge Rule, Call-Outs, and Check-Backs.

SBAR - was designed as a tool for communicating critical information that requires immediate attention and action concerning a patient's condition. It is also widely used as part of patient handoffs. **Situation:** What is going on with the patient? **Background:** What is the clinical background or context? **Assessment**: What do I think the problem is? **Recommendation and Request:** What should I do to correct it?

The Two-Challenge Rule - requires the communicator to voice their concern at least twice to receive an acknowledgment by the receiver. This rule is invoked when a healthcare team member suggests or performs an intervention that deviates from the standard of care. The nurse would assertively voice their concern at least two times. If the team member who is challenged does not acknowledge this concern, the leader would then take a stronger action or utilize the hospital chain of command as needed.

Call-Outs - is a strategy that leaders can use to inform all team members of crucial information during emergencies to help team members anticipate what comes next.

Check-Backs - require the sender of the communication to verify the information received by the other team member or use closed-loop communication.

Build a Patient-Centered Culture

An effective strategy to ensure quality and safety is to create a patient-centered culture on your team. A patient-centered culture is built on the principles of compassion, service, and high quality. Team members plan their actions and behaviors based on what is best for the patient. The patient experience becomes paramount. Hospitals that don't provide a quality patient experience, along with quality care, inherently struggle with deteriorating reimbursement rates, as well as low scores on the Hospital Consumer Assessment of Healthcare Providers and Systems (HCAHPS) Survey.[12] The long-term effects of these reimbursement declines can be detrimental to a hospital's fiscal health and may make sustaining the mission impossible.

Creating a positive experience goes beyond meeting a certain standard of health care—it has to do with the entire patient journey, from the first interaction with the patient to the very last. Creating a patient-centric culture requires every person in the organization to approach every decision with the mindset of "how will this impact the patient experience?" Nurse leaders can use this approach to reinforce compliance with best practices such as bedside shift report. Bedside shift reports and rounding by the team are an essential part of improving communication with patients and families. Patients and loved ones are anxious to hear status updates about their prognosis. Whether the news is good or bad, the more clearly and more frequently, healthcare professionals communicate, the better the experience will be for the patient. Yet, many nurse leaders find mixed staff compliance with the consistent practice of bedside report. It should be presented as a must-do activity that needs to be part of team culture rather than a decision that an individual team member can make.

PERFORMANCE METRICS

The patient experience metric measured by the HCAHPS survey described above is one of many performance metrics tracked in healthcare environments to measure quality and safety. Nurse leaders today are often overwhelmed with the relentless focus on performance metrics tracked on unit dashboards. These KPIs (key performance indicators) vary in importance across clinical settings. Examples of key metrics related to nursing care include:

- Patient satisfaction scores
- National patient safety indicators
- Nursing sensitive outcome measures such as CAUTI, patient falls, pressure ulcers, hours of care per patient day, ventilator-associated pneumonia.
- Hospital-acquired conditions
- Nurse turnover
- Patient throughput

When Chelsea took a medical-surgical nurse manager position, she felt inundated with the volume of reports she received on quality indicators measured on her unit. Her hospital is Magnet-designated and participates in sending information to the National Database of Nursing Quality Indicators® (NDNQI).[13] Chelsea receives reports that compare the performance of her unit to similar units across the country. Researchers at Press Ganey have found that nurse managers like Chelsea at the unit level exert substantial influence on the work environment of nurses at the bedside and, ultimately, on performance across measures of safety, quality, and patient experience, as well as indicators of nurse engagement, such as nurse job satisfaction and retention.[14] Chelsea's director suggested that she focus on five key measures that are recurring problems on the unit. She also recommended that Chelsea review some of the best practices of leaders on the highest performing units in the NDNQI database. These included the following:[14]

- Use RN-led shared governance teams to review performance metrics and recommend practice changes.
- Conduct regular leader rounding.
- Involve all team members in unit decision-making.
- Eliminate shift rotation.
- Support full nurse participation in interprofessional teams.
- Connect with staff in a caring manner.
- Use huddle boards as visual evidence of quality improvement progress.
- Promote bedside reporting, whiteboards, hourly rounding, and communication.
- Nurture a nonpunitive, just culture.
- Reward RNs for reporting errors and engage them in improvement initiatives to prevent repeats.

Just Cultures

The last two best practices outlined above remind us that even with a diligent focus on patient safety and quality, errors happen in clinical environments. In the previous two decades, healthcare organizations have moved from punitive action on all errors to a just culture approach. The just culture model acknowledges that humans make mistakes, and because of this, no system can produce perfect results.[15] Given that premise, human error, and adverse events should be considered outcomes to be measured and monitored with the goal being error reduction (rather than error concealment) and improved system design.

The just culture model describes three classes of human behavior in error occurrence. The first is simple human error, inadvertently doing something other than what should have been done. The second, at-risk behavior, occurs when a behavioral choice made increases risk. It could be that risk is not recognized or is mistakenly believed to be justified. The third, at-risk behavior, is an action taken with conscious disregard for a substantial and unjustifiable risk.

Adopting a just culture approach establishes an organization-wide mindset that positively impacts the work environment and work outcomes in several ways. A just culture promotes a process where mistakes or errors do not result in automatic punishment, rather the goal is to uncover the error source. Errors that are not deliberate or malicious result in coaching, counseling, and education around the error, ultimately decreasing the likelihood of a repeated mistake. Errors are evaluated and managed based on which class of human behavior is present—reckless conduct results in disciplinary action. When nurse leaders work in just cultures, most errors are handled in a less punitive way. When a just culture is embraced in a healthcare setting, it improves patient safety, reduces errors, and gives nurses and other health care workers a significant stake in the improvement process.

EVIDENCE-BASED PRACTICE

Nurse leaders play a crucial role in ensuring that the best evidence is used in clinical practice settings. Clinical care based on the best evidence is safer, increases reliability, and improves outcomes. Unfortunately, there are gaps in the use of evidence-based practice, and in some settings, it is a low priority. [16] Beth found this problem when she took a position as a nurse manager in a critical-care unit. Based on her experiences in other settings, she was surprised to learn that the ICU had a restrictive visitation policy. Only two adult immediate family members had access to the ICU twenty-four hours a day for ten minutes every hour, and visits were between 0730-0830 and 1500-1600. Children could not visit. Only the nurse manager or supervisor could approve exceptions to the policy.[17]

Before Beth's arrival, several nurses attempted to implement a less restrictive visitor policy but met pushback from nurses who desired more restrictions. Beth reviewed the evidence with her staff. In 2016 the American Association of Critical-Care Nurses issued a practice alert that called for unrestricted presence and participation of a support person in adult intensive care units.[18] Under Beth's leadership, the ICU visitor policy was revised to supported open visitation using the best available evidence. She educated staff about the changes and developed a monitoring system to track compliance at one month, three months, and six months. Had she not insisted on the policy change, it is highly unlikely that the visitation practices would have changed.

KEY POINTS

✓ Excellent patient outcomes occur in cultures where there is a relentless focus on safety and quality.

✓ A culture of zero-tolerance for bullying is the most effective leadership strategy to prevent its occurrence.

✓ One of the most robust ways to ensure quality and safety is to create a patient-centered culture on your team.

✓ Creating a patient-centric culture requires every person in the organization to approach every decision with the mindset of "How will this impact the patient experience?"

✓ The just culture model acknowledges that humans make mistakes, and because of this, no system can produce perfect results.

CHAPTER 13

PROMOTING STAFF ENGAGEMENT

A strong predictor of team performance is the level of engagement of team members. Vicki Hess is an employee engagement expert. She developed an engagement formula: *Satisfied + Energized + Productive at Work = Employee Engagement.*[19] *Satisfied* is when you are psychologically connected with the work. *Energized* means you are willing to put effort into your work. *Productive* means that our efforts contribute to the organization's overall vision and bottom line and it is verifiable. There is a strong business case for staff engagement. The Gallup Corporation has studied engagement for over three decades. There are strong relationships between the engagement of a team and the achievement of key performance indicators such as the following: [20]

- Reduced turnover
- Lower absenteeism
- Reduced medical errors

- Patient loyalty
- Improved staff well-being
- Higher productivity

Today, most organizations routinely track staff engagement (some even quarterly) with assessments such as the Gallup Q-12, the Glint survey, or Press Ganey workforce engagement solutions. Unfortunately, their findings indicate that most organizations have an employee engagement problem. The Gallup organization reports that only about 33% of the US workforce is engaged in their work.[21] The Nursing Advisory Board has studied nursing engagement and noted that only about 32.8% of the professional nursing workforce are engaged at work, and 7.4% are actively disengaged.[22] Leadership approach, workload, organizational change level, decision latitude, and career opportunities impact engagement levels and job stress. Research done by the Gallup Organization indicates that managers account for 70% of employee engagement variance.[3] US managers are only slightly more engaged in their work than their staff. Engagement starts with you, the leader. If you are not engaged in your work, it will be impossible to engage staff. You need to walk the talk of engagement and know what drives engagement. In their current engagement data, Glint researchers found four key drivers of engagement:[23]

1. The ability to learn and grow in the work setting
2. A positive work culture with few or no toxic behaviors
3. Trust in leaders
4. Having a voice that is listened to

Sometimes the level of staff engagement changes when there are stressors in the environment. Erica experienced this in her unit during the COVID-19 pandemic. During the third and fourth quarter of 2020, the Glint engagement scores on her team dropped into the zone of concern. The scores dropped in two key areas, the first was staff feelings of empowerment, and the second was recognition of their contributions. Erica worried this might happen because the staff was negative about frequent policy changes during COVID – some staff complained that they no longer felt valued. Shared governance was more challenging with social distancing. Erica was disappointed with the findings but did not make excuses about it being a crisis. Unless she confronted the problem, there would be no improvement. She was determined to improve staff engagement and was transparent with staff about the findings. Erica reviewed the evidence on staff engagement and some of the following key leadership strategies to enhance engagement: [23]

1. **Reconnect staff with their purpose.** Erica recognized that the experience of COVID-19 had been challenging for her team. Many were so stressed and fearful that they forgot about what matters most to them in their work. She encouraged staff to share their stories and take pride in what they had accomplished.

2. **Create psychological safety.** In discussions with staff, Erica understood that COVID had shaken some staff's core beliefs about how safe they were at work. She worked hard to keep her team in their circle of influence and talk about what was in their control.

3. **Rebuild trust.** During COVID, there were many policies and practice changes in response to the challenges with the virus. These changes led staff to question whether their leaders knew what they were doing. Erica acknowledged these feelings but reminded staff that no one had ever been through anything like COVID before.

4. **Reinvolve staff in unit governance.** Staff participation in shared governance had decreased during COVID. Erica restarted the unit practice council. Their initial project was to look at ways to improve staff engagement.

5. **Provide intentional recognition.** Erica understood how staff might not feel appreciated. The organization's annual nurse recognition day was canceled in 2020 and not rescheduled. Erica was determined to be more intentional in recognizing staff.

6. **Provide development activities.** During COVID, staff education programs were suspended. Professional development before COVID was robust, and staff missed these educational opportunities. Erica planned development activities for the team. She also advocated for an organizational recommitment to development. She scheduled a coaching session with each staff member to set goals for the upcoming year.

Engagement as a Shared Responsibility

While Erica is responsible for building a culture to promote staff engagement, the responsibility is not hers alone. Work engagement is a two-way street. Vicki Hess contends that a crucial part of the puzzle often missed in evaluating work engagement is the employee. She has observed that it has become OK for staff to say that they are not engaged in their work through media messages.[19] Individual employees may not see that they, too, have a responsibility in the engagement process.

Marshall Goldsmith, in his book *Triggers,* notes that questions on some engagement survey instruments deepen this problem by framing employee engagement as an organizational responsibility.[24] A reason for variance sometimes seen in employee engagement is that some staff naturally accept it as a personal responsibility while others do not. To foster engagement, Erica needs to promote the idea that it is a shared responsibility by encouraging disengaged staff to ask themselves the following questions:

1. Did I do my best to set clear goals today?
2. Did I do my best to finding meaning in my work today?

3. Did I do my best to be happy today?
4. Did I do my best to build positive relationships today?
5. Did I do my best to be fully engaged today?

These questions encourage the idea of action learning as part of the engagement process by emphasizing a need for ongoing growth and reflection.

EMPOWER SHARED GOVERNANCE

The involvement of team members in unit or department decision-making is a crucial driver of engagement. Shared governance is a model of participatory decision-making.[25] Nurses meet through practice councils or other forums to decide clinical practice standards, quality improvement, staff and professional development, and research. The model incorporates a commitment to the value of shared decision-making among critical stakeholders about issues that affect one's work. In some organizations, the shared governance structure is very robust and includes the nursing staff's elected president. The design may be more informal in other organizations, but it usually includes unit practice councils, committees, and task forces. Shared governance may look different in different settings, but the outcomes are the same: a feeling of having been heard and included in decisions that directly impact us whenever possible.

Nurse leaders play a vital role in how successful shared governance is in an organization. Staff will disengage from shared governance if they are not empowered by their leaders to drive change. The shared governance process needs strong staff involvement but requires leader support. It is a developmental partnership to promote the right structure and processes so councils can work effectively independently.[26] Here are some dos and don'ts.

The Dos

- Familiarize yourself with your organization's shared governance model.
- Clarify for council members their role, responsibilities, and scope of authority.
- Coach staff to develop the leadership skills necessary for shared governance.
- Give staff time to research and plan initiatives.
- Help in the scheduling of council meetings.
- Schedule staff so they can attend shared governance meetings.
- Involve the council in providing input for leadership decisions.
- Carefully consider all initiatives and ideas that come from shared governance structures.
- Recognize staff who are engaged in shared governance.
- Be a Yoda and listen much more than you talk.

The Don'ts

- Do not take charge of the shared governance efforts in the unit or department.
- Do not shut down ideas even if you are unsure of their feasibility.
- Do not deny requests of staff to participate in critical planning meetings.
- Do not be Superman or the advice monster and try to add too much value.
- Do not be critical of staff efforts in shared governance.
- Do not ignore or fail to respond to requests from shared governance committees.

The success of shared governance in clinical settings hinges on the leader's ability to lead a shared decision-making environment effectively.

When you embrace the power of shared governance, it will result in both higher staff engagement and the development of future leaders.[27]

WHEN TEAM MEMBERS LEAVE

Losing valued members of an engaged team is hard. If not managed well, it can lead to other staff disengaging. A wise mentor once told me that a resignation should be viewed as a funeral. *"How you behave – she observed – is a tribute not only to the person leaving but to everyone left behind."* I have always found this to be good advice. Once a staff member has decided to resign, regardless of how inconvenient it is for you as the leader, how you behave says a great deal about you. It impacts how honest employees on your team will be with you if they consider other career opportunities and whether you are someone who supports professional growth. Staff may choose to resign for many reasons, some of which you will have no control over. Leaders who feel that a resignation indicates disloyalty acquire a reputation as angry and vindictive. Managing resignations with grace is a necessary leadership behavior. Your leadership behaviors should include the following:

- Acknowledge their contributions to the team and that they will be missed.
- Ask if there is anything you can do to change their mind (if you want to).
- Work with them on a transition date and any benefits they may be entitled to.
- Keep the lines of communication completely open.

Your team will carefully watch how you respond when someone leaves. Do you demonstrate grace and gratitude, or do you behave in a way that seems angry and reactive? Ultimately, for your unit or department's good, you want your staff member to feel good about the workplace and ready to recommend it to others who might be interested. If you stay in your leadership role long enough, you may even be surprised at how many staff often return to their former positions when they find out the grass is not greener somewhere else.

Many employers now have active strategies to contact staff who have left and invite them back. Nurse leaders who do not already do this should strongly consider the five following ways that they can leave the door open for team members to return:

1. Before the staff member leaves, sit down with them, and wish them the best. End the conversation by saying that sometimes new positions do not work out, and if this happens, to please call. Do not criticize the new employer.
2. Leave a great last impression by giving them a going away party and thanking them for their contributions to the team.
3. Ask to connect with the staff member on LinkedIn – this will allow you to see how they are progressing in their career and send congratulatory messages.
4. Do not hold grudges against staff who leave and speak highly of them to their co-workers who probably stay in touch with them.
5. Send holiday messages and if the staff member has had a major tragic life event – reach out.

How you manage staff who leave speaks volumes about your leadership to the rest of your team. It is natural for a team to feel a sense of loss and even grief. If you lose a staff member, keep in mind that it does not have to be forever. Unfortunately, great supportive leaders are in short supply, but staff often do not realize this until they leave. Leave the door open so they can come back.

KEY POINTS

✓ Research done by the Gallup Organization indicates that managers account for 70% of employee engagement variance.

✓ Work engagement is the responsibility of both the organization and the individual staff member.

✓ Nurse leaders play a vital role in how successful shared governance is in an organization.

✓ How you manage staff who leave speaks volumes about your leadership to the rest of your team.

CHAPTER 14

MANAGING RESISTANCE TO CHANGE

Today's healthcare environment is characterized by volatility, uncertainty, complexity, and ambiguity. At no time was that more apparent than during the recent COVID pandemic. Policies and practices changed daily as new information became available from the Centers for Disease Control, the World Health Organization, and various state agencies. This change pace was challenging for nursing staff, and many leaders dealt with negativity and resistance to change. Resistance to change is not surprising. We are often asking staff to make significant changes to their practice with new policies or initiatives. When a change occurs, new behaviors need to be learned, and old behaviors must be unlearned (Figure 10).

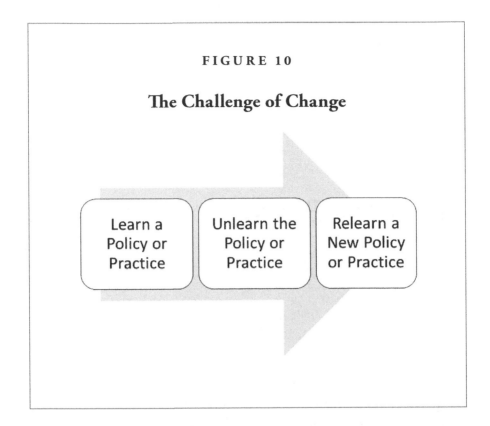

FIGURE 10

The Challenge of Change

Learn a Policy or Practice → Unlearn the Policy or Practice → Relearn a New Policy or Practice

These changes are difficult because our practices are, in essence, a collection of habits. Charles Duhigg, an investigative reporter for the New York Times, wrote an interesting evidence-based book about how habits are formed and what we can do to change them.[28] Duhigg contends that habits make up 40% of our daily routines, whether at work or home. What you see in your work environments are habits that develop over time. Habits are the brain's way of saving energy. They allow us to work on autopilot. A mistake that leaders make is that they forget how ingrained habits are. Hardwiring a new habit can take more than the 30 days we often devote to implementing new initiatives. Therefore, change can be so challenging. It is also the reason why experienced staff may have more challenges with change than novices. Practice habits become hardwired over time. Any new habit or practice, especially one that involves new learning like technology shifts, may feel threatening to a nurse who sees herself as an expert. Significant changes can make staff feel psychologically unsafe because the brain perceives it as a threat.

MEET STAFF WHERE THEY ARE

You have probably noticed that not all staff accept change in the same way or on the same timeline. In his work on the diffusion of innovation, Everett Rogers discovered that acceptance of innovation or change is on a bell curve (Figure 11).[29]

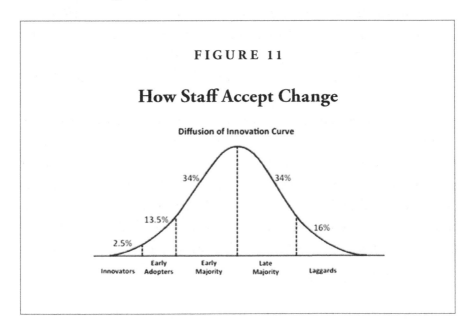

FIGURE 11

How Staff Accept Change

Diffusion of Innovation Curve

Some nurses are natural innovators or early adopters. Other staff will be slow to adopt change. Nurse leaders need to meet people where they are in the change process. Changing parts of one's practice can be quite emotional. It often means letting go of something that you have valued in the past. During times of rapid change, staff can feel psychologically unsafe. Your team depends on you to help them understand the meaning of the change – why is it needed, and how will it impact them. The language that leaders use to frame change has significant consequences for the way individuals make sense of the world and their actions. The heart-head-hands messaging discussed in Chapter 6 is essential to convey a sense of urgency in a change. Most nursing staff understand that the costs, fragmentation in care, and variable outcomes in today's system are not sustainable moving into the future.

You will observe distinct behavioral patterns in how staff responds to change. Kerry Bunker identifies four different ways that staff respond to change (entrenched, overwhelmed, poser, or learner).[30] Entrenched staff may decide that they outlast change, for example - *"Maybe it will not happen until I retire."* Karen had this problem in her primary care clinic. It was full of what she described as CAVE dwellers or staff who are **C**onsistently – **A**gainst – **V**irtually – **E**verything. Driving change with her team is a struggle.

Overwhelmed staff have high anxiety levels during a time of change and may have feelings of depression or powerlessness. Posers exhibit a high level of confidence in their ability to deal with changes but may not have the self-awareness and actual competence that they need. Learners feel challenged and stretched but are determined to move forward. They seek learning opportunities to expand their skills in response to the change. Learners can be a leader's best ally in helping other staff transition during changes.

In a time of change, we are often substituting the new and unfamiliar for the old. Some changes will be perceived negatively by staff. In Chapter 6, we discussed how to message bad news. You need to be clear about why the change is needed and the background behind the decision. You can give staff time to vent but not debate the decision. The timeline for the change is nonnegotiable. Once you have done that, shift the discussion to the future.

There are always possibilities in change that can lead to a new, brighter future, which should be discussed. Leaders who remain calm, truthful, and optimistic in their communications help to prevent the spread of misinformation and reduce staff anxiety. There are silver linings in almost any situation, and the leader needs to be the first to help everyone see what they are. An optimistic attitude and outlook on the part of the leader can be very energizing and contagious. It will motivate your staff to do their best. You need to expect success if you are to achieve it.

PLAN CHANGE INITIATIVES

Great ideas and initiatives can and do fail when leaders do not strategically plan change initiatives. As we learned with a crisis like COVID-19, strategic priorities can quickly shift in today's environment. Leaders need to be very agile in their ability to manage change, but it is still essential to take the time to ask the following four questions:

Is the timing right for the change?
John Maxwell identified the law of timing as one of his *21 Irrefutable Laws of Leadership*. [31] He observed that timing is often the difference between success and failure in implementing initiatives. Sometimes the organizational climate may not be ready for new initiatives or change. When units experience a great deal of upheaval, change fatigue can set in. Sometimes great ideas cannot gain traction in organizations because there are too many competing factors in the environment. It is crucial to explore what these competing factors are before moving forward.

Have I created the conditions for success?
To effectively implement a new initiative, staff in an organization need to understand why it is required. You need to tell the compelling story of why change is necessary. Sometimes new leaders bring successful

initiatives from other organizations but fail because they may not be directly transferable to an organization with a different culture.

Have I involved staff in planning?

Staff and unit practice councils need to be involved in the planning process to create buy-in. Passive resistance from some staff is not lethal in small doses, but it leads to a crippling slowdown of the change effort over time. You need a team of champions who support the change and will help drive it. Carefully plan with your team how, when, and where to educate staff about the initiative. A lecture may not be the right strategy when the change calls for new skills that need to be practiced and observed.

Have I established a process to make it stick?

Initiatives need to be embedded in the culture to be successful. Paradoxically, change leaders often focus all their efforts on the "upstream" issues of getting change through the starting gate and then wonder why an initiative stalls after a few months.[32] A successful early drive is rarely sufficient to overcome internal resistance and people's longing for the "old ways" – whether or not these old ways serve their best interests.

Successful leaders are strategic planners who understand that the building blocks need to be in place for initiatives to succeed. Leaders need to realize that the initial change platform they create is only valid for a short time. They need to conserve their energy to confront the problematic issues that will stem from passive resistance and the unpredictable side effects that change creates. Leadership is critical at every stage of the change process. You cannot let up. Nurse leaders sometimes complain about the lack of staff compliance with practices like bedside shift reports, yet the problem is that we do not build in mechanisms to hardwire changes into practice. Wise leaders know that they must also create a culture that reinforces the new habit by making it stick.

To be successful, this may include changing rewards and recognition to influence the development of new behaviors.

RESPOND TO CHANGE FATIGUE

Each new workplace change, whether it be practice changes, leadership changes, technology upgrades, or a merger with another health system, requires time, effort, energy, and adaptation. It is not surprising that periods of upheaval can easily cause change fatigue at both an individual and organizational level. We sometimes forget that change comes at a cost when the cumulative effects of change can lead to staff feeling depleted. Anna, a critical-care nursing director, experienced this problem in her unit during COVID-19. Policies and practices changed almost daily in response to a surge of patients during the pandemic. During the initial phases of the crisis, her staff responded heroically and were agile in their willingness to change. As the pandemic continued, she saw change fatigue set in. Her team started to become cynical and angry with each new change.

Anna's experience was not unusual. During a crisis, it is difficult to pace changes to avoid change fatigue. David Altman, a change management expert, advises leaders to take the following steps when they see change fatigue setting in to promote change energy:[33]

1. Work to prioritize your change efforts and focus on those initiatives that have the highest priority. Avoid changing anything that does not need to be changed.
2. Recognize and talk about the reality that all change is the beginning of something new and the end of something old that was previously best practice.
3. Teach staff evidence-based resilience strategies and stress management practices to deal with ongoing change in the environment.

4. Build a culture of psychological safety so staff can speak their truths about what they are experiencing.

As a nurse leader, you will not always be able to control the pace of change. You can help your team become more resilient with the strategies we will discuss in Chapter 15. Anna did when she focused the energy of her team on what they could control in the face of massive change. Anna understood that some staff struggled more than others with the pace of the change. She individualized her coaching with staff members and met them where they were. Anna also recognized the need to be transparent in her communication and not dismiss the critical care staff's concerns. Leadership visibility and proactivity are crucial in combatting change fatigue.

KEY POINTS

- ✓ New behaviors need to be learned when change occurs, and old behaviors must be unlearned.
- ✓ Not all staff accept change in the same way or on the same timeline.
- ✓ Great ideas and initiatives can and do fail when leaders do not strategically plan change initiatives.
- ✓ During a crisis, it is difficult to pace changes to avoid change fatigue.
- ✓ As a nurse leader, you will not always be able to control the pace of change. What you can do is to help your team become more resilient.

CHAPTER 15

FOSTERING INDIVIDUAL AND TEAM RESILIENCE

Even before COVID-19, there was great concern about the level of stress and burnout nurses reported. In the whitepaper, "The IHI Framework for Improving Joy in Work", the authors noted that if burnout in healthcare were described in clinical or public health terms, it might well be called an epidemic.[34] Dr. Donald Berwick, the former CEO of the Institute for Healthcare Improvement (IHI), observed that it seems paradoxical in healthcare where caring is the focus, that so many healthcare professionals experience burnout and a loss of joy in their work. A 2019 whitepaper on clinician burnout from the National Academy of Medicine estimated that between 35% and 54% of US nurses have substantial burnout symptoms.[35]

As the COVID-19 crisis illustrated, preventing burnout, and promoting nurse resilience has never been more critical. Reported well-being among nurses plummeted during the crisis, and the repercussions are likely to be felt for a long time. Nurse leaders play a crucial role in helping staff to adapt to changes in their environments, reduce burnout, and build a resiliency muscle. It is often nurse leaders who are the first to see the signs of burnout in their staff. These symptoms include the following:[36]

- Chronic exhaustion and insomnia
- Profound negativity
- Overwhelming irritability
- Disengagement from work
- Resistance to change
- Loss of empathy
- Physical symptoms (GI symptoms, headaches, chronic pain, immunosuppression)

When Grace assumed leadership of a COVID-19 unit during the crisis, she began to see the above signs of burnout in her staff. She looked at the research on burnout and designed interventions which included the following:[36]

1. Scheduling changes to ensure adequate time off between shifts.
2. Temporary redeployment of staff with acute symptoms to less stressful areas.
3. Assignment of routine breaks for staff with coverage for nutrition and hydration.
4. Monitoring use of vacation time to ensure staff was taking them.
5. Designation of a quiet room for staff breaks on the unit.
6. Incorporation of gratitude for what is going well into the safety huddles.
7. Resiliency coaching for staff.
8. Weekly check-ins with every staff member to see how they are doing.
9. Use of Code Lavender when the team reaches their emotional limits.

On one particularly stressful day when many patients had died, Grace could see her team was intensely grieving. She utilized the Code Lavender® intervention that had recently been implemented in her health system.[37] The Code Lavender is an integrative healing equivalent of a Code Blue and is designed for staff support in a crisis. Evidence-based relaxation and restorative interventions like prayer and facilitated conversation are provided to help staff meet their immediate responsibilities and debrief about the situation.

THE EVIDENCE ON RESILIENCE

Grace's goal in utilizing the interventions above was to promote staff resilience. Resiliency helps us to bounce back from stressors and serious challenges in our lives. If we want our staff to have long and productive careers, it is important to help them develop resiliency. As a leader, you will never be able to eliminate all the stresses and challenges in the work environment. When staff are more resilient, they have the strength to tackle their problems head on and manage adversity with less stress. How we view adversity and stress strongly impacts our capacity to bounce back. Martin Seligman, a psychiatrist and national expert on resilience, believes that reframing how we explain setbacks to ourselves is the key to developing resilience.[38] Situations are rarely as good or bad as we may describe them. The stories that we tell ourselves about what is happening can either promote resilience or increase our stress level. To promote our resilience, it is essential to stop ruminating about the stress that we feel. When you are resilient, you recognize that both positive and negative expeiences can lead to transformational growth.

When working with her team members to promote resilience, Grace noted that her youngest staff had the highest levels of stress and anxiety. This is not surprising. Personal resiliency is deeply rooted in the habits of our mind as much as our values and beliefs. It is shaped by our personal experiences with adversity, our natural levels of optimism, the level of impact that an experience has on our lives, our social support system, and our propensity to ruminate.[38] Grace's seasoned staff had more experience with adversity in their lives, and their well-being and resilience was higher. Nurse well-being studies conducted during the pandemic supported Grace's observations with younger staff reporting significantly lower levels of well-being.

In research conducted prior to COVID-19, the American Psychological Association reported that young Millennials and Generation Z had higher levels of both *trait anxiety* and *state anxiety*.[39] *Trait anxiety* is our baseline anxiety level. The increased baseline anxiety levels of both these generational cohorts has been linked to the rise of social media. When a nurse has a naturally high trait anxiety level and is then placed in a stressful situation, it can result in diminished resilience. The good news is that resiliency is like a muscle, it grows as we learn to successfully navigate negative situations. We can also promote our own resilience by adopting evidence-based activities such as those below:[40]

- Seeking support from family and friends
- Exercising especially in outdoor venues
- Increasing our hours of sleep
- Adopting a healthy diet
- Journaling what we are grateful for
- Engaging in leisure activities such as reading, music or baking
- Reducing our time on social media
- Practicing yoga or meditation

Resiliency strategies are not one size fits all. Some nurses love yoga and meditation, but others do not. Some will find solace in sharing their experiences with their colleagues. Others have found less screen time to be helpful.

Coaching to Promote Resilience

When Grace observed some of her staff struggling with their resilience during COVID, she began doing individual and team resilience coaching. One tool (see toolbox Part 5) that she found effective was helping staff stay in their circle of influence. During COVID, Grace's team often asked her questions such as the following:

- Is my job secure?
- Is our health system financially healthy enough to sustain low revenues?
- Will we have enough PPE if there is a resurgence?
- Is it safe for me to continue working?
- When will patients come back and seek services again?
- When will things go back to normal?

These questions were hard to answer because of the level of uncertainty. Grace's goal with the staff was to help them be more resilient. She encouraged them to ruminate less often over things they do not have control over and spend their time on things that are within their circle of influence. The late Dr. Stephen Covey first proposed the Circle of Influence versus the Circle of Concern in his book, *Seven Habits of Highly Effective People.*[41] Dr. Covey points out that if we want to be proactive in a crisis rather than reactive – we will focus on the things we can control, also known as our circle of influence. We need to let go of those that we cannot influence but are in our circle of concern. We care about these things. We may worry about them, but we cannot control them.

When coaching staff who are in a crisis, you want to help them to look at goals that are part of the circle of influence as Grace did. For example, we cannot control the reality that this is a stressful time. Still, we can learn to manage our behaviors in response to stress – such as through nutrition, exercise, sleep, meditation, and maintaining a positive attitude. We also know that we are more resilient when we take actions that benefit others — not only our patients but one another. Some great coaching questions to ask to promote resiliency include the following:

1. What impact is your stress having on your well-being?
2. What have you done in similar situations when you felt stressed?
3. What actions are you taking to maintain optimism currently?
4. What personal behaviors do you have that could be contributing to your stress and anxiety?
5. What personal changes do you need to make?
6. What needs to be true that is not true today for you to be more resilient?
7. Who could support you at this time in your home environment?
8. What will happen if you do nothing and continue to be stressed and scared?

RESILIENCE AFTER A LIFE-QUAKE

Throughout our lives, we experience transitions such as births, deaths, marriages, or new jobs. These transitions can have a significant impact on our roles, responsibilities, assumptions, and routines. Some life events fall into a different category and are called life-quakes. COVID-19 is an excellent example of a life event that became a global life-quake. In his book, *Life is in the Transitions*, Bruce Feiler describes a life-quake as a massive life change that is high on the Richter scale of consequences and has aftershocks for years.[42] When people experience life-quakes, their top two emotions are fear and sadness. Nurse leaders saw these emotions in their staff as everyone came to grips with the reality that the future will not be like the past. The pandemic will change most of us in different ways. The experience challenged some of our core beliefs in nursing. Most nurse leaders assumed there would be a strong national response to a pandemic. We thought there would be readily available protective equipment for staff. We may have believed we could always protect staff and allay all their fears. We might have expected that the public would listen to science. We presumed that health systems would be busy and not have financial challenges in a pandemic. Many of our beliefs turned out not to be accurate. At this point, we are all still trying to make sense of the experience.

The good news is that life-quakes do not last forever. We will transition through it in three phases (Figure 12).[42] The first phase is the long goodbye. In this phase, you realize that you need to let go of some aspects of the past. Sometimes, we can get stuck in grief over what we have lost. The second phase is the messy middle. This messy middle can last for an extended time, and it is hard. During this phase, we shed habits, routines, and beliefs that no longer work for us. During this messy middle, we can be at our creative best because we need to be to heal. The final phase is a new beginning. Life-quakes serve as an important reminder that none of us lead linear lives. Transitions will always be part of life, and some will be massive.

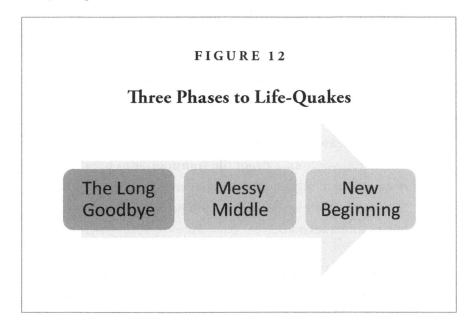

FIGURE 12

Three Phases to Life-Quakes

The Long Goodbye — Messy Middle — New Beginning

Resiliency coaching during a life-quake is incredibly challenging. Marcus experienced this in his perioperative leadership role. During COVID-19 surges, most elective surgeries were postponed. The OR staff were either furloughed or redeployed to other areas. His team became cynical and disillusioned. For many months, they were in the first phase of the long goodbye. They experienced many losses, including certainty about their job stability, loss of faith in their health system to protect their safety, and a belief that the public would follow the science during the pandemic. There was grief about things that changed in everyday life. Marcus studied the evidence on how to best coach his team through this life-quake.[43] He designed a plan that included the following steps:

1. **Help the team recalibrate.** Many things changed in their health system and lives as an outcome of COVID. Marcus asked his team to list their core beliefs and assumptions before COVID that had now changed. He gave them time to grieve these losses.

2. **Help the team reframe the experience.** Marcus found in their initial discussion; staff focused on the negative aspects of the experience. He understood from resilience work that the stories we tell ourselves about our experiences are powerful. He challenged his team to identify how they had grown and new things they had learned as a team.

3. **Help the team use the experience to help others.** A powerful way to recover from a major life transition is to use their experience to serve others. Marcus challenged his team to develop ideas to take their lessons learned and prepare future perioperative nurses for pandemics.

Marcus coached both the team and some individual staff members that were struggling. He was especially concerned about an experienced

OR nurse named Mia. She had worked in the OR for 15 years before COVID. During COVID, she was redeployed to a medical-surgical unit. She was still angry and depressed about the experience. During her annual review, she told Marcus that she was considering leaving nursing, commenting that *"I did not sign up for what happened and never want to go through that again."* Marcus coached Mia using the same steps above that he used with the team. He asked some powerful questions to help Mia gain perspective on the experience, including the following:

- What has changed about the way you approach life?
- What is the story of what has happened to you?
- What is the real challenge for you in this experience?
- Do you have new or different priorities today than you did before?
- When you have encountered life transitions before – how did you cope with them?
- What have you learned about yourself during this life-quake that you did not know?
- Where would you like to go from here in your life?
- What would need to be true that is not true today for you to move through this transition more successfully?
- How can I best support you as your leader?

Marcus was not sure whether Mia would change her mind about leaving nursing. The coaching goal was to help her reflect on her experience and make the best life decisions moving forward.

KEY POINTS

✓ Between 35% and 54% of US nurses have substantial symptoms of burnout.

✓ If we want our staff to have long and productive careers, it is essential to help them develop resiliency.

✓ When coaching your team in a crisis – you want to help them look at goals within their circle of influence.

✓ A life-quake is a massive life change that is high on the Richter scale of consequences and has aftershocks for years.

PART 3 REFERENCES

1. Maxwell J. *The 17 Indispensable Laws of Teamwork: Embrace Them and Empower Your Team.* New York: Harper Collins; 2013.
2. Grubaugh ML, Flynn L. Relationships among nurse manager leadership skills, conflict management and unit teamwork. *Journal of Nursing Administration.* 48(7), 383-388; 2018.
3. Clifton J, Harter J. *It's the Manager.* New York: Gallup Press; 2019.
4. Department of Veterans Affairs (2020). A guide to performance-based interviews Available at https://www.va.gov/pbi/questions.asp
5. Christfort K, Vickberg S. *Business Chemistry: Practical Magic for Crafting Powerful Team Relationships.* New York: Wiley Publishers; 2018.
6. IPEC. Core Competencies for Interprofessional Practice 2016. Available at https://www.ipecollaborative.org/core-competencies
7. General David Morrison Quote Available at https://en.wikiquote.org/wiki/David_Morrison
8. Tye J, Dent B. *Building a Culture of Ownership in Healthcare.* Indianapolis: Sigma Theta Tau; 2020.

9. Rehder J. et al. Associations between a new disruptive behaviors scale and teamwork, patient safety, work-life balance, burnout and depression. *The Joint Commission Journal on Quality and Safety.* 44: 18-26; 2020.

10. Thompson R. *Enough: Eradicate Bullying and Incivility in Healthcare.* Incredible Messages Press; 2019.

11. Team STEPPS ® Pocket Guide App 2018. Available at https://www.ahrq.gov/teamstepps/instructor/essentials/pocketguideapp.html

12. HCAHPS: Patients' Perspectives of Care Survey ND Available at https://www.cms.gov/Medicare/Quality-Initiatives-Patient-Assessment-Instruments/HospitalQualityInits/HospitalHCAHPS

13. NDNQI 2020 Press Ganey https://www.pressganey.com/resources/program-summary/ndnqi-solution-summary

14. Press Ganey. 2017 Special Report: The Influence of Nurse Manager Leadership on Patient and Nurse Outcomes and Mediating Effects of the Work Environment. Available at https://www.pressganey.com/resources/white-papers/2017-nursing-special-report

15. ANA Just Culture Position Statement (2010) Available at https://www.nursingworld.org/~4afe07/globalassets/practiceandpolicy/health-and-safety/just_culture.pdf

16. Caramanica L., Ford LG. Establishment of Nurse Manager Leadership Competencies to Support Clinicians in Evidence-Based Practice: A Delphi Study. Association of Leadership Science in Nursing 2020 Virtual International Conference.

17. Milner K, Kean L. Evidence-Based Practice Scenario. Presented at the National QSEN Conference. Bonita Springs, Fl; 2018.

18. American Association of Critical Care Nurses. (2016). AACN Practice Alert Family Visitation in the Adult Intensive Care Unit. Available at https://www.aacn.org/clinical-resources/practice-alerts/family-presence-visitation-in-the-adult-icu

19. Hess V. 6 *Shortcuts to Employee Engagement.* Vicki Hess; 2013.

20. Gallup 2020. Employee engagement and performance: Latest insights from the world's largest study. Available at https://www.gallup.com/workplace/321032/employee-engagement-meta-analysis-brief.aspx

21. Harter J. (October 2020). U.S. Employee Engagement Reverts Back to Pre-COVID-19 Levels. https://www.gallup.com/workplace/321965/employee-engagement-reverts-back-pre-covid-levels.aspx

22. Advisory Board 2014. The national prescription for nurse engagement: best practices for enfranchising frontline staff in organizational transformation. Available at http://www.advisory.com/research/nursing-executive-center/studies/2014/national-prescription-for-nurse-engagement

23. HR Research Institute Glint Sponsored Work. The state of employee engagement and experience 2020. Available at https://www.glintinc.com/resource/the-state-of-employee-engagement/#:~:text=The%20State%20of%20Employee%20Engagement%20in%202020.%20Things,Employee%20Engagement%20and%20Experience%20in%202020%20to%20learn%3A

24. Goldsmith M. Triggers: *Creating behavior that lasts, Becoming the person you want to be.* New York: Crown Business; 2015.

25. Porter-O'Grady T. Principles for sustaining shared/professional governance in nursing. *Nursing Management. 50*(1), 36-41; 2019.

26. Guanci G. The nurse manager's role in a shared governance culture. *Nursing Management.* 49(6), 46-50; 2018.

27. Hancock B, Meadows MT. The nurse manager and professional governance: Catalysts for leadership development. *Nurse Leader.* 18(3), 265-268; 2020.

28. Duhigg, C. *The Power of Habit: Why We do What We do in Life and Business.* New York: Random House; 2012.

29. Rogers E. *Diffusions of Innovation 5th Edition.* New York: Free Press; 2003.

30. Bunker K A. In Rush. S. (Editor) *On Leading in Times of Change.* Greensboro, N.C.: Center for Creative Leadership; 2012

31. Maxwell J C. *The 21 Irrefutable Laws of Leadership*. Nashville: Thomas Nelson Publishers; 2007.

32. Beaudan E. (January/February 2006 Ivey Business Journal). Making change last: How to get beyond change fatigue. Available at MAKING CHANGE LAST: HOW TO GET BEYOND CHANGE FATIGUE • (iveybusinessjournal.com)

33. Altman D. (September 4th, 2020 Center for Creative Leadership Blog). Ditch change fatigue and embrace continual evolution. Available at https://www.ccl.org/blog/change-fatigue-continual-evolution/

34. IHI Joy in Work Whitepaper. (2017). Available at https://www.ncha.org/wp-content/uploads/2018/06/IHIWhitePaper_FrameworkForImprovingJoyInWork.pdf

35. National Academies of Sciences, Engineering, and Medicine 2019. Taking Action Against Clinician Burnout: A Systems Approach to Professional Well-Being. Washington, DC: The National Academies Press. Available at https://doi.org/10.17226/25521.

36. Kelly C. (American Association of Critical Care Nurses Blog June 25th, 2020). A focus on the positive fuels resilience and prevents burnout. Available at https://www.aacn.org/blog/a-focus-on-the-positive-fuels-resilience-and-prevents-burnout

37. Stone SB. Code lavender: A tool for staff support. *Nursing 2018*. 48(4), 15-17.

38. Seligman M. Building resilience. *Harvard Business Review*. 89(4):100,106,138; 2011.

39. American Psychological Association. Stress in America: Generation Z 2018 Available at https://www.apa.org/news/press/releases/stress/2018/stress-gen-z.pdf

40. Mind Tools. Developing Resilience: Overcoming and Growing from Setbacks. Available at https://www.mindtools.com/pages/article/resilience.htm

41. Covey SR. *The 7 Habits of Highly Effective People*. Simon & Schuster; 1989.

42. Feiler, B. Life is in the Transitions: Mastering Change at an Age. New York: Penguin Press; 2020.
43. Tedeschi RG. Growth after trauma: Five steps for coming out of a crisis stronger. *Harvard Business Review.* 2020:127-131.

PART 4

LEADING IN ORGANIZATIONS

*"How do leaders earn respect in organizations?
By making sound decisions, by admitting their
mistakes, and by putting what's best for their
organization ahead of their personal agendas."*

JOHN MAXWELL

CHAPTER 16

UNDERSTANDING HEALTHCARE REIMBURSEMENT

Most purchases that we make in our daily lives are relatively straightforward. You know the price of the item or service, make a payment, and then receive the service. The transaction is transparent and may take only minutes. Healthcare purchases are a major exception to these norms of everyday life. The final price of a service is not billed until after it is provided, and the payment system is convoluted. Consumers can leave the hospital or a provider's office without any idea of the final bill. Payment of the invoice could take months, and full payment by an insurer is often not guaranteed. Not surprisingly, consumer frustration with the healthcare delivery system is high, and health policy around reimbursement is always a priority political issue.

Healthcare costs in the United States are among the highest globally, yet patient outcomes are often not as good.[1] Even within the US, there are wide geographic disparities in the cost of care. Our traditional payment methodology is a significant contributor to healthcare's overall cost in this country. Under the historical fee-for-service reimbursement model, the incentive is to do more to be paid more. Payment incentives are quickly moving away from this volume-oriented approach toward a greater focus on the value of services and health outcomes, including fewer hospitalizations. As we move into the future, consumers are likely to demand much more price transparency at the point of service. Hospitals and providers will assume more risk and need to ensure that the services are low cost and high quality. The many performance measures tracked in every area of patient care, such as hospital readmissions, patient falls, and patient satisfaction will continue to have a significant impact on reimbursement in a value-focused environment.

Changing payment models, regulatory requirements, cost containment pressures, and disruptive competition are among the significant challenges facing leaders in today's health care environment.[2] Regardless of whether your organization is governmental, for-profit, or not-for-profit, nurse leaders need to understand the essentials of healthcare reimbursement. Without adequate reimbursement for services and a disciplined approach to controlling costs, organizations cannot meet their mission. A perineal concern for all healthcare leaders is learning to do as much or more with decreasing resources. To be transformative in your nursing leadership, you need to have a clear understanding of the reimbursement system and the impact on the bottom line of your organization. The more you know about healthcare financing and financial terminology, the more confident you will be in negotiating for scarce resources.

Jorge learned this in his first year as a manager of an orthopedic unit. His health system participated in the Center for Medicare and Medicaid (CMS) Bundled Payments for Joint Replacements. Jorge was part of a hospital-wide committee that examined the costs for care for both hip and knee replacements. Although he was a novice leader, it surprised him that even more experienced team members had so little knowledge about these patients' actual care costs. It was an excellent learning experience for the team to examine what they were currently spending and consider cost reduction opportunities. Jorge saw that as a nurse leader, his efforts in managing the inpatient care of joint replacement patients could either contribute positively to the economic bottom line or increase the risk that the bundled reimbursement would not cover actual costs.

Payer Mix in Healthcare

The population you serve and who pays for their care plays a crucial role in healthcare reimbursement. You can have two patients on a unit with the same diagnoses but vastly different reimbursement levels for their care, depending on what has been negotiated by the payer. Nurse leaders should know their patient mix (age and diagnoses), the payer mix (who pays for care), and their case mix index (CMI). A unit's profitability is measured by the case mix index calculated by weighing the profitability of the diagnoses using the Diagnostic Related Group (DRG) of discharged patients.[3] A CMI of 1.0 means your costs are average. A high CMI (above 1.0) indicates that the unit cares for a higher acuity patient population who receives more big-ticket services resulting in more patient revenue. All three of these metrics have a direct impact on the organization's bottom line. The major payers for services in healthcare fall into the following classifications:[4]

- **Medicare** – Patients 65 or over who are part of the Medicare Program. Medicare patients average 21.8% of the payer mix in most health systems, but this could be far higher in areas with retirees.
- **Medicaid** – Patients with lower incomes that qualify for their state Medicaid programs or are part of Medicaid Advantage plans. On average, these patients are 12.8% of the payer mix nationally but much higher in the Western states.

• **Private/Self/Others** – Patients who have private commercial insurance, are self-pay, have no insurance, or are on Medicare Advantage plans. These patients are, on average, 66.5% of the payer mix nationally.

Commercial insurance usually pays more for health care services than government plans do. Many hospitals depend on that private insurance differential to stay afloat. With information about the payer mix of patients on your unit, you can be strategic as you examine reimbursement changes such as a reduction in Medicare or Medicaid. Even when patients have insurance, it is not uncommon to for them to have policies with high deductibles for their care. These high deductibles may be challenging for the patient to meet and can result in bad debt for your institution. If you work in a safety net hospital where many patients are uninsured, financing care will always be a high priority for the leadership.

Payment Systems

Healthcare systems in the United States deal with more than 1,600 different insurers. Each insurer has different plans and often unique requirements for hospital bills. Add to that decades of government regulations, which have made a complex billing system even more complicated and frustrating for everyone involved. No one expects nurse leaders to be experts in hospital finance and billing, but it is essential to have some basic understanding of the following three payment systems:

Prospective Payment by DRG
More than three-quarters of the nation's inpatient acute-care hospitals are paid under the inpatient prospective payment system. The payment amount for a particular service is derived based on the classification system of that service. For inpatient hospitals, this classification is known

as the Diagnostic Related Group or DRG. Under prospective payment, hospitals are paid a flat rate based on the average charges across all hospitals for a specific diagnosis, regardless of whether an individual patient care costs are more or less. Everything from aspirin to an artificial hip is included in the package price to the hospital. How much is paid for a DRG depends on whether the payer is Medicare, Medicaid, or a private insurer. Nurse leaders should be aware of the top five diagnoses of patients admitted to their areas by requesting a list of DRGs from their billing office. Knowing this information allows you to proactively consider the impact on unit revenue when substantive changes in lengths of stay and reimbursement for specific diagnoses occur.[3]

BUNDLED PAYMENTS

The use of bundled payments is growing in popularity among healthcare payers because it requires care coordination by all providers. A single, comprehensive price is negotiated that covers all the services involved in a patient's episode of care. These episodes can include a wide range of conditions from maternity care to hip replacements, cancer, and organ transplants. So, for example, if the expected cost for an uncomplicated hip replacement is $10,000, then reimbursement would be at that level whether the episode costs more or less. Bundled payments can align incentives for providers – hospitals, post-acute care providers, physicians, and other practitioners – and encourage them to work together to improve the quality and coordination of care. Orthopedic care reimbursed by Medicare is one of the most popular areas for bundled payment.[5]

FEE FOR SERVICE (FFS)

The fee for service reimbursement model is the traditional and most commonly used payment model in outpatient settings. In this model, healthcare providers charge based on individual services rendered (i.e., appointments, treatments, tests ordered, prescriptions written). Bills then list out these services separately, often making them long and complicated.

Under FFS reimbursement, a physician's revenue is based solely on what procedures they perform. Each individual "service" a patient receives would have a corresponding code (ICD-9 codes) with a price attached. For example, a 15-minute office consult, a tetanus shot, a urinalysis, and a basic metabolic panel all have different codes and fees attached to them. FFS reimbursement approaches are referred to as "volume-based" reimbursement because providers' primary way to increase their revenue is to increase the number of services they perform.[3]

Value-Based Care

Value-based programs reward health care providers with incentive payments for the quality of care to those covered under Medicare. These programs are part of a broader quality strategy to reform how health care is delivered and reimbursed. Health systems are rewarded when they can avoid costs associated with problems like patient falls, infections, or readmissions. Three value-based care programs that nurse leaders have direct involvement with include:

1. **The Hospital Value-Based Purchasing Program (VBP)**
   This program seeks to improve patient safety and experience by basing Medicare payments on the quality of care provided rather than on the number of services performed. Hospital VBP affects payment for inpatient stays in more than 3,000 hospitals across the country. Under this program, Medicare rewards hospitals with fees based on either how well they perform on specific quality measures or how much they improve their performance. These bonus payments are funded by a 2% reduction in all payments. Hospital VBP is budget neutral. The entire 2% reduction is paid back to participating hospitals. The highest-performing hospitals can earn back bonuses

more generous than the payment reduction, while others may receive minimal payment increases or not earn a bonus payment at all. Hospitals are assessed on outcome measures such as the following:[6]

- Mortality and complications
- Healthcare-associated infections
- Patient safety
- Patient experience – HCAHPS
- Process
- Efficiency and cost reduction

2. THE HOSPITAL READMISSION REDUCTION PROGRAM

This program is a Medicare value-based purchasing program that encourages hospitals to improve communication and care coordination to better engage patients and caregivers in discharge plans and, in turn, reduce avoidable readmissions. The excess readmission ratio (ERR) is used to assess hospital performance. The ERR measures a hospital's relative performance and is a ratio of the predicted-to-expected readmissions rates. Unplanned readmissions are those that occur within 30 days of discharge for patients. When readmissions occur before 30 days, a payment readjustment penalty can be applied to all Medicare discharges. At this time, the following types of discharges are monitored under the program: [7]

Acute myocardial infarction

Chronic obstructive pulmonary disease

Congestive heart failure

Coronary artery bypass graft surgery

Elective total hip arthroplasty or total knee arthroplasty

3. THE HOSPITAL-ACQUIRED CONDITIONS REDUCTION PROGRAM

This is a Medicare program that encourages hospitals to improve patients' safety and reduce the number of conditions people experience from their time in a hospital, such as pressure sores and hip fractures after surgery. CMS adjusts payments when documented hospital-acquired conditions exceed what is expected. The payment reduction is for all Medicare fee-for-service discharges in the corresponding fiscal year. The following are examples of conditions that are monitored by CMS and subject to reimbursement penalties:[8]

- Patient falls
- Pressure ulcers
- Postoperative sepsis
- Central line-associated bloodstream infection (CLABSI)
- Catheter-associated urinary tract infection (CAUTI)
- Methicillin-resistant staphylococcus aureus (MRSA) bacteremia
- Clostridium difficile infection (CDI)

Reimbursement penalties in these value-based programs can significantly negatively impact an organization's bottom line, especially when your payer mix includes a large percentage of Medicare patients. When this happens, nurse leaders may be asked to join committees or task forces to look for ways to reduce the problems leading to lower reimbursement.

Taylor had that experience in her role as a medical-surgical manager. The payer mix on her unit was 85% Medicare. Her health system struggled with a high rate of readmissions among patients with congestive heart failure. Taylor served on a care coordination committee that worked closely with home health agencies and nursing homes in her community to reduce readmissions. They devised some innovative programs, including follow-up discharge visits by acute care nurses on Taylor's unit. She demonstrated over time that these visits sharply reduced hospital readmissions and improved the organization's bottom line.

HEALTH POLICY AWARENESS

Health policy changes can have a significant impact on healthcare reimbursement. Nurse leaders should be attentive to proposed policy changes and consider their impact on their clinical setting. Two important contemporary examples include proposed changes to the Affordable Care Act (ACA) passed in 2010, and the current discussion about Medicare shortfalls. ACA is an excellent example of a policy initiative that has both strong support and strong opposition. The law has four primary goals: [9]

- Make affordable health insurance available to more people by creating a Health Insurance Marketplace. It prevents insurance companies from denying coverage due to pre-existing conditions and requires plans to cover a list of essential health benefits.
- Provides consumers with subsidies ("premium tax credits") that lower costs for households with incomes between 100% and 400% of the federal poverty level.
- Expand Medicaid to cover all adults with income below 138% of the federal poverty level. (Not all states have expanded their Medicaid programs.)
- Support innovative medical care delivery methods designed to lower the costs of health care generally.

When the law passed, it contained an individual mandate that required everyone to have health insurance or pay the penalty. That has since been eliminated. During the 2020 election, ACA was again an issue with calls to have it overturned. Most in the healthcare industry support the act. The availability of coverage through healthcare exchanges set up as part of ACA has sharply reduced the number of uninsured Americans and unpaid bills. The ACA's future remains uncertain, but healthcare leaders agree that any substitute needs broad coverage to ensure health systems' sustainability.

Unlike other industries where payment is expected at the time services are provided, billing in healthcare occurs after care is received, and reimbursement is not guaranteed. Health systems often carry large amounts of bad debt due to nonpayment. In 1986, Congress enacted the Emergency Medical Treatment & Labor Act (EMTALA) to ensure public access to emergency services regardless of ability to pay. Hospitals that participate in Medicare have to provide an appropriate medical screening examination (MSE) to anyone seeking treatment for a medical condition, regardless of citizenship, legal status or ability to pay.[10] Participating hospitals may not transfer or discharge patients needing emergency treatment except without the informed consent or stabilization of the patient or when their condition requires transfer to a hospital better equipped to administer the treatment. EMTALA does not guarantee healthcare equity but has prevented the historical practice of moving acutely ill, often compromised patients to overwhelmed safety-net hospitals. When large numbers of Americans are uninsured, they are still entitled to emergency care under EMTALA whether or not they can pay. As a nurse leader, it is vital to understand your health system's level of bad debt. Although it is unusual for hospitals to go bankrupt, some do and may even close.

Even with the movement to value-based care, there is concern about the Medicare program's sustainability. Without a significant change in the funding strategy, the Medicare Hospital Insurance Trust fund will be insolvent in 2026. Medicare's cash shortfall is currently responsible for one-third of the federal debt.[11] It is not exactly clear what will happen if the trust fund were to become insolvent because it has never happened before. Any solution moving forward will likely involve a combination of tax/premium increases and a decrease in healthcare reimbursement. These changes could significantly impact all health systems, with more than 20% of patients currently covered by Medicare. This is one health policy issue that needs to be on the radar of every nurse leader.

KEY POINTS

✓ Payment incentives are quickly moving away from a volume-oriented approach toward a greater focus on the value of services and health outcomes, including fewer hospitalizations.

✓ You will hear three terms during unit budget reviews: *patient mix, payer mix, and case mix index.*

✓ Value-based programs reward health care providers with incentive payments for the quality of care to those covered under Medicare.

✓ Reimbursement penalties in these value-based programs can significantly negatively impact an organization's bottom line, especially when your payer mix includes a large percentage of Medicare patients.

✓ Without a significant change in the funding strategy, the Medicare Hospital Insurance Trust fund will be insolvent in 2026.

CHAPTER 17

LEARNING BUDGET BASICS

M ost nurse leaders readily admit that understanding finance and budgeting is the most challenging part of the role.[12] It is a vital competency and one that you will need to advance your career. Tara was in her third month as nurse manager of a busy Level 1 trauma unit. She gained confidence in most aspects of her new role but confided in her mentor that she still felt very insecure about the mastery of her financial responsibilities. With some humor, Tara acknowledged that she has problems balancing her checking account and is now accountable for a 12-million-dollar budget. Her mentor reminded her that when she started nursing school, some subjects like pharmacology and anatomy seemed like a foreign language at first. But over time, as she gained experience, the terminology in these two subject areas seemed natural.

Like math phobia, you can overcome a fear of budgeting when you invest the time to become more financially savvy. Nursing is the largest professional group within the hospital and usually the most expensive. We play a vital role in helping to reduce costs. Over the next decade, there will be many changes in healthcare delivery. Nurse leaders contribute to the strategic planning of new programs. Critical to planning new projects is to understand how to project revenue and budget for expenses. Key expectations of nurse leaders in most settings in budgeting include the following:

- Participate in the preparation of the unit/department annual budget.
- Track budget variances.
- Educate staff about unit budget issues.
- Monitor the use of supplies and routinely evaluate supplier cost and unit stock.
- Track performance measures linked to the amount of revenue received.
- Maintain and prevent damage to equipment in the unit or department.
- Watch for long-term trends in your unit's patient-to-staff ratios to avoid overstaffing or understaffing.
- Know your options for per diem staffing if your unit regularly needs it and know the budget ahead of time.
- Limit excessive use of unscheduled leave.
- Track and resolve issues that contribute to overtime.
- Ensure nursing hours do not exceed the target number of hours per patient day (HPPD) or hours per modality if in an ambulatory setting.

Nurse Unit/Department Budgets

A budget is nothing more than a plan to manage resources. Surprisingly, there is little uniformity in nursing budgets across organizations. The budget categories may be similar, but cost centers, processes, and accountability for the budget are often different. As a new leader in an organization, it is crucial to understand your specific responsibilities in the budgeting process. Some areas to pay attention to include the following:

The Budget Cycle -A budget cycle is the timeframe that a yearly budget covers. Some organizations use the calendar year from January to December. Others use a fiscal year beginning in July and ending in June. Federally funded healthcare organizations use a fiscal year that begins October 1st and ends in September. Budget development for the next year usually starts at least six months before the current year's budget expires. Most nurse leaders participate in budget planning and make forecasts about staffing, supplies, and equipment.

Different Types of Budgets – Organizations have more than one type of budget. Your *operating budget* is your day-to-day expenditures. This budget includes the revenue your area generates and the expenses, including labor, supplies, and pharmacy costs. Your *capital budget* is your equipment needs or replacement needs for longer-term investments such as IV pumps, patient beds, or point of care testing equipment. This budget is separate from your operating budget, and items are usually over a certain dollar amount, such as $1000. If you lead a specialty program such as hemodialysis, you may also have a *program budget* to cover all the needs of patients across the organization. A program budget focuses careful attention on both the program's costs and the value to the organization.

Cost Centers – Your unit or department is usually broken down into one or more cost centers that accumulate costs and generate revenue. For nurse leaders that supervise multiple units, each area will probably have its cost center report that outlines budget and variances. These cost center reports can be very confusing for new leaders. You will want to review which personnel are in your cost center and what equipment and supplies. Beginning leaders should take these cost center reports to a more senior leader in nursing or finance and review the report line by line. Sometimes cost centers are charged for years for services that are no longer part of patients' care. Nurse leaders are accountable for variances in their cost centers, so developing expertise in this area will make you much more effective in your leadership.

Interdepartmental Charges - These are charges for supplies and services from other departments such as phlebotomy, pharmacy, and central supply.

Average Length of Stay– ALOS is the number of patient days in each period divided by the number of discharges in that period. The budget is calculated on the ALOS of patients on the unit – not the outliers.

Fixed Costs – These costs do not change in total as volume changes, i.e., you need a unit clerk, a housekeeper, a nurse manager.

Variable Costs – These costs vary in direct proportion with your patient volumes, such as staffing, pharmacy, and supply costs.

Nurse Staffing – The Biggest Part of the Budget

All organizations have some fixed costs that do not vary with a patient census. These costs would include things like utilities, insurance, mortgages, and telephones. A much larger part of the budget is variable costs that change according to patient volume and activity. The single most significant variable cost in healthcare organizations is staffing. That is why staffing costs in any organization are closely monitored. Nurse leaders need to be familiar with the following metrics around staffing:

Acuity – This is the measurement of patient severity of illness related to the amount of nursing care resources required to care for the patient. For example, based on patients' acuity on your medical-surgical unit, you may plan 4 hours of direct nursing care per patient day.

Unit of Service/Volume – UOS is the measure of activity that defines the unit workload. This is determined by the number of inpatients admitted to an inpatient bed by the midnight census on most units. In an emergency department, it would be the patient visits per day.

Hours per Patient Day (HPPD) – This is the budgeted standard of productive, direct care hours for inpatient units. Many health systems determine uniform HPPD as benchmark goals for various specialty areas or patient populations. It is essential to ask questions about whose time is in the HPPD. Does the HPPD only include RNs providing direct care to patients or other staff members such as educators and managers also part of HPPD? When there are variations in the HPPD on a unit, the nurse leader usually needs to prepare a variance report to explain why the unit is either overstaffed or understaffed on a particular shift relative to patient volume. You may need to do this on a monthly, weekly, or even a daily basis, depending on your organization. The HPPD may not account for patient activity levels, such as a high volume of admissions, discharges, or transfers. If you work in an ambulatory setting, productivity measures may be calculated on procedures performed or patient encounters, such as hours per modality (HPM).

Full-Time Equivalent (FTE) – FTE is generally based on 40 hours a week or 2080 hours per year. If a staff member is full-time, they are equal to 1 FTE. A half time employee is .5 FTE. You might have 60 FTE in your core staffing, but the actual number of nurses you employ can be far greater when you have part-time staff. FTE core staffing levels are usually allocated based on historical patient volumes and acuity.

Productive and Non-Productive Time – Productive time in most organizations is the direct care hours staff care for patients. Non-productive time includes all paid time off, family medical leave, and jury duty. You will need to know where activities like orientation, mandatory training, and meeting times are placed in your organization's productivity hours.

Overtime – Overtime is generally considered any work over the 36 or 40 contracted hours per week, but this is variable across organizations. Any work beyond the standard 8, 10- or 12-hour tours is considered overtime in some settings. Excessive overtime wreaks havoc on unit budgets. Nurse leaders need to closely monitor the use of overtime to assess for patterns of use, such as routine overtime for charting at the end of a shift. It is usually more cost-effective to use a per diem staff instead of paying overtime. The widespread use of sitters to monitor patients on a 1:1 observation presents unique challenges for leaders in controlling overtime and staffing costs.

Other Staffing Costs - Shift differentials, on-call pay, per diem staff and travel contracts are also part of the unit budget.

Staffing Mix – This is your staff's composition, including RNs, CNAs, LPNs, and unit Secretaries. Skill mix is the competency level and scope of practice of various staff members.

When nurse leaders have budget overruns, it is usually the result of staffing decisions. Chapter 18 will take a closer look at strategies to improve staff scheduling and reduce turnover. Budget overruns in a unit budget usually need to be justified through variance analysis. Nicole had this challenge with her critical care budget. Six of her experienced staff were selected for positions in a new cardiac intervention unit. The new unit was a high priority strategic program for her health system. Nicole had only one month's notice to find staffing replacements. Few experienced critical care nurses applied for the unit vacancies. Nicole knew that she would need to "grow her own" ICU staff, but this would take time. She hired three travel nurses for three-month contracts to stabilize her staffing mix. These travel contracts were an unplanned budget expense, and she had to prepare a budget variance report to justify the change.

MONITOR THE USE OF SUPPLIES AND EQUIPMENT

Nurses are often unaware of costs in their inpatient or outpatient settings, especially equipment and supplies. Medical supplies account for up to 17% of total hospital expenses.[13] Reducing supply use can have a significant impact on a unit budget. Inventory management refers to the overseeing and controlling the ordering, storage, and use of supplies that a hospital or other healthcare organization will use in the provision of care. Many health systems now work to control costs by avoiding the stocking of too many supplies that may not be used and become outdated. New leaders quickly learn that there is an art to this supply chain management. If too many supplies are ordered, some will remain unused and become outdated. When too few supplies are ordered, the just in time supplies ordered to fulfill the need are often more costly. Nurse leaders in procedural areas or the operating room are usually more involved with ordering supplies and medical devices. One of the highest costs of inventory in a hospital is the operating room. In most operating rooms, surgeons have a procedure card for each type of surgical procedure that the respective surgeon performs. The procedure cards list all the items or inventory required for the procedure.

The current direction of supply-chain management in healthcare is to standardize supplies across health systems. The price of supplies and equipment are usually lower when there is group buying. At the unit level, you may have no input into the selected supply vendors, but there are other ways to manage your supply budget. Excessive use of supplies or a failure to scan supplies can quickly add up and impact a unit or department's budget. Likewise, when supplies and equipment are not readily available, excessive nursing time is spent on what is described as "hunting and gathering" activities. New managers can gain some early wins by determining what types of supplies are often missing on units, causing staff frustration. This also avoids the phenomenon of hoarding of supplies on a unit by the nursing staff. The Cleveland Clinic has saved tens of thousands of dollars in a "just do it" project initiative designed to eliminate the waste on units when staff place supplies in their pockets to save time.[13] Frontline staff can provide invaluable information about supply use.

The cost of medical equipment has skyrocketed over the past decade. Not surprisingly, most pieces of equipment may now fall into the capital budget category. Any capital budget request requires strong justification. You are competing with other demands in your organization. Nurse leaders need to be strategic about their wish lists. Keeping a firm grasp on the condition of equipment on the unit is essential. Chapter 4 discussed nurse leader rounding, which could include asking staff questions about equipment and supplies. Often, staff may assume you know that a piece of equipment is not working when you may not. When evaluating equipment, you may need to assess whether it should be leased or bought. If your recommendation is to purchase it, the committee may want to know about its depreciation value. If, as an example, you request the purchase of a portable fetal monitor that costs $10,000, and the estimated life is five years, the depreciation value would be $2,000 per year. For any new equipment purchase, you may be asked to do a return on investment as outlined below.

CONDUCTING A RETURN ON INVESTMENT

When you evaluate a return on investment with equipment, you measure the amount of return or savings that can be achieved by the purchase, relative to the cost. In a nursing capstone project, Lale Johnson, a clinical nurse leader, did an interesting return on an investment analysis involving the purchase of additional Dynamap (vital sign) machines for her medical-surgical unit.[14] With only three functional Dynamaps, nurses were waiting for each to start their rounds. She estimated that it took each of the 47 RNs on the unit 15 minutes (twice each shift) to find an available machine. She calculated the total average waste of RN time to be 264 hours, or $17,100 monthly and $188,100 annually. She proposed the purchase of four additional Dynamap machines costing $12,812 in total. Her return on investment included diverting some of the 264 hours of RN time saved to establish a more effective system to reduce supply waste. She also contended that the purchase of new Dynamaps would help decrease staff frustrations and stress, leading to staff turnover. Finally, the delay in starting bedside rounding impacted the patient experience and the unit HCAHPS scores.

The request that Lale laid out for the capital budget committee was well thought out. She realized that just saying it would save RN time would not be enough. She had to consider how that regained time would be spent, and the organization's possible positive outcomes.

KEY POINTS

- ✓ Like math phobia, fear about budgeting can be overcome when you invest the time to become more financially savvy.
- ✓ The budget is your organization's plan to coordinate their financial goals.
- ✓ The single most significant variable cost in healthcare organizations is staffing.
- ✓ Medical supplies account for up to 17% of total hospital expenses.
- ✓ When you evaluate a return on investment with equipment, you measure the amount of return or savings that can be achieved by the purchase, relative to the cost.

CHAPTER 18

MANAGING YOUR
STAFFING RESOURCES

C hapter 17 reviewed budgeting basics. The largest expenditure in any healthcare unit or department budget is staffing. It is one area where nurse leaders can both improve productivity and reduce costs. Staffing should be planned to ensure that there is an effective match between patient needs and nurse competencies. What constitutes appropriate nurse staffing is a debatable topic. The current evidence on nurse staffing suggests that an increase in nurse staffing is related to decreases in risk-adjusted mortality, nosocomial infection rates, surgical patients' complications, development of pressure ulcers, readmission rates, and failure to rescue.[15] Poor staffing is associated with nursing burnout, stress, work-related injuries, and turnover. What is true of all of the research is that no "ideal staffing level" has been identified.[16] California was the first state to mandate nurse staffing, but their ratios were from expert consensus and not evidence-based work.

Therese Fitzpatrick, a staffing expert, points out that future staffing will be much more scientific and evidence-based. Big data analytics will be key and allow leaders to look at staffing in real time.[17]

A significant percent of the time of frontline leaders is spent on staffing and scheduling issues. Many health systems use consensus panels to determine nursing care hours per patient day based on the specialty area's average acuity. Nurse leaders should justify their staffing ratios with evidence from their own patient encounter data in the electronic medical record, from the literature and specific data on how staffing impacts patient outcomes. This justification is not always easy to provide because numbers alone do not tell the whole story. There are five qualitative factors in any organization or on any unit that also need to be considered:[18]

1. **The organization and work rules** - The type of organization can make a difference. Staffing needs may differ in academic settings where nurses work closely with house staff to coordinate care versus a community hospital where there is a stable hospitalist group. Some organizations establish work rules that impact scheduling such as the number of tours a nurse can work consecutively or weekends off each month.

2. **The patient population** - Units or organizations with a higher case mix of older patients may require different staffing than organizations with a younger population, even with the same patient acuity. Some patient populations are at higher risk for falls, infections, and pressure ulcers. Expectations about nursing involvement in discharge planning also need to be considered.

3. **Support services and architectural layout** – The level of ancillary support an organization provides will impact the RN staffing needs. Are nurses expected to answer the phone and do the transport of patients? The geographical layout of a unit can make the work of nurses either easier or more demanding. Patients today expect private rooms but depending on the features and

design of those rooms – it may increase staff work and an RN's ability to assume the care of additional patients.

4. **Daily census and unit turnover** - A considerable amount of nursing work is spent on admissions, transfers, and discharges. The volume of these ADTs may not be reflected when a patient census is taken once a shift.

5. **Staff expertise and competency** – Nurse expertise and competence should be considered when staffing a unit. Departments with a higher percentage of new graduates may need more staffing.

To some extent, the perception of adequate staff is in the eyes of the observer. You may have two nurses working on a unit, and one feels it is very understaffed while the other feels that the workload is manageable. Staff involvement in staffing and scheduling is critical.[18] Nurse staffing and productivity committees can be an excellent way for organizations to evaluate their own unique needs. Nurse leaders at the frontline need to have a hands-on approach relative to staffing. It is critical to monitor key areas like overtime use, sick leave, and the skill mix on each shift. Many staffing decisions occur when the manager is not present, so it is also essential to educate charge nurses about productivity metrics and staff coverage costs.

Sometimes when leaders move to a new position, they discover patterns in scheduling or resource use that drive up costs without contributing to patient care. That happened to Paige when she became director of an emergency department (ED). She was recruited to the position because she was a seasoned leader with strong budget experience. The ED had three interim leaders over five years. During her first 100 days, she evaluated the unit scheduling and interviewed staff. She found the following issues in how staffing resources were managed:

• Nurses routinely clocked out fifteen minutes after their shift was over to finish their documentation resulting in thousands of dollars in overtime each month.

- No mid-shift staffing adjustments were made in the ED by charge nurses resulting in frequent staffing variances due to increases or decreases in patient volume.
- Sick leave usage was often linked to the beginning or end of planned vacations.
- When staffing was short, the default plan was to call in agency nurses, which cost the facility more money than per diems or staff working overtime.
- ED nurses worked overtime as sitters in the ED for patients who had overdosed instead of using the EMTs who could cover these responsibilities.
- There were three full-time travelers scheduled in the ED who worked for more than nine months with no specific recruitment plan to fill these positions.
- The department RN turnover was 21% the previous year with a $92,000 average replacement cost.

Paige's findings are not unusual. When resources are not closely monitored, expenses increase, and productivity declines. Paige was transparent with the ED team about the issues with staffing resources. She first tackled the overtime and sick leave use. She worked with the charge nurses to examine more cost-effective ways to cover gaps in the schedule. Paige encouraged the charge nurses to schedule in blocks of time shorter than 8 or 12 hours to avoid productivity variances. She began active recruitment for the positions filled by travelers and evaluated how sitters were scheduled and used. Lastly, she studied the issues impacting turnover with hopes of decreasing it by at least 50%. There are no easy solutions to staffing problems, and the answers may not be universal. In today's healthcare environment, managing staff productivity is a delicate balance between meeting the patient needs for care and maintaining fiscal responsibility. We are likely to see smaller numbers of core staff on units and broader use of highly skilled float or flex pools in the future.[17]

MANAGE STAFFING VARIANCES

Nurse leaders like Paige quickly learn how staffing variances can negatively impact a unit budget. Staffing budgets are planning tools to manage resources based on the best projections available. Staffing plans are constructed based on expectations about unit patient volumes, acuity level, staffing mix, and staff involvement in non-direct care activities. A variance occurs when there is a difference between what is budgeted versus the expenses incurred. Sometimes, variances are favorable when fewer staffing resources are used, but more often staffing exceeds projections. Staffing variances can occur for a variety of reasons, including the following:

- Patient volumes do not meet projections.
- Staffing mix – a higher number of new graduates.
- The acuity of patients is higher than anticipated.
- Regulatory changes occur that result in increased or decreased care.
- An increase in the number of patients requiring close observation.
- Lack of availability of internal staff to meet needs.
- An increased volume in admissions/discharges and transfers.
- Changes or introduction of technology that involves more staff time.
- Unanticipated new staff training costs.
- Changes in the practices of admitting physicians.
- Staff illness or increase use of family medical leave (FMLA).

The variance analysis helps the nurse leader understand unit staffing problems. Armed with this knowledge, the nurse manager can take corrective action. Nurse leaders need to be attentive to any changes in the environment that might impact staffing. This was a lesson learned during COVID when patients' acuity was higher than typically seen in critical care and on medical-surgical units. Other unique factors during the pandemic, such as time spent donning and doffing PPE and time spent contacting families, were not factored into 2020 nursing unit staffing budgets.

Unionized Environments

Nurse leaders who work in unionized environments have additional considerations to pay attention to when staffing and scheduling. According to the Bureau of Labor Statistics, 20.4% of nurses belong to a collective bargaining unit.[19] When nurses are unionized, they work under a contract negotiated with the health system. These bargaining agreements generally have provisions in them about staffing resources, which could include any of the following:

- The posting of position vacancies and the selection process
- Seniority rights of staff relative to leave, days off, or holidays
- The ability to allow staff to self-schedule
- Mandatory and voluntary overtime
- Acuity based staffing systems
- Use of agency nurses
- Redeployments and floating
- Furloughs
- Scheduling requests
- Notification about scheduling
- Requests for leave
- Provisions for continuing education

Nurse leaders are usually exempt from union contract coverage. If your hospital has a negotiated agreement, you should know what is in the staff contract and adhere to all the requirements. When a leader fails to comply with some aspect of the agreement, a grievance may be filed against them. The negotiation of grievances costs time and money.

Jasmin, a new leader, learned this lesson the hard way. One of her Labor and Delivery nurses requested every Wednesday off to attend her RN-BSN program. Jasmin granted the request and began to incorporate it into her staffing plan. She later learned that five other nurses were also in the same education program and needed the same day off. Three nurses had seniority in the role, which gave them the first right to request the day off per their union contract. Jasmin could only guarantee the Wednesday off to the nurses with seniority. This caused conflict in the unit, and two of the nurses eventually left their positions. Jasmin learned from this experience to use the contract to guide her discussions with staff, something she had not been required to do in non-union settings.

THE HIGH COST OF NURSE TURNOVER

A key area of concern in staffing today is the management of nurse turnover. Alex assumed a management role in a surgical intensive care unit that had lost 10 RNs the previous year. The average ICU nurse replacement cost was $92,000, including recruitment, onboarding, and supplementary staff use for scheduling until the vacancy was filled. The total turnover costs were just short of $1,000,000. While Alex knew he could not eliminate turnover, the goal of reducing it by 50% would be a cost savings of almost $500,000. These numbers can quickly add up in large health systems, which is why unit turnover needs to carefully be carefully monitored.

For more than a decade, we have known that changes in the nursing workforce's demographics would eventually lead to shortages. Pre-COVID staffing data in 2020 indicated a 9% national nursing vacancy rate.[20] COVID-19 accelerated the retirements of many Baby Boomer nurses. New graduates or nurses with just a few years of experience are replacing some very seasoned staff. This phenomenon is a second type of nursing shortage that the Nurse Advisory Board describes as the

experience-complexity gap.[21] Competition for experienced perioperative, ICU, emergency room, and labor and delivery nurses, along with other specialties, has grown. Many new graduates now accept acute care positions to work for one to two years and then return to graduate school. Leaders want to support their staff's career goals, yet they are stressed by knowing that patient safety and quality are at stake. The employment landscape for nurses has changed, as have the career goals of younger staff. The following are some of the new realities in nurse staffing that confront today's leaders:

1. Working in specialty units such as ED, ICU, and L&D have been popularized in the media as being cool places to work. New graduates seek these roles right out of nursing programs.
2. Hospitals often put a "one year until transfer to another unit" policy to combat unit turnover, only to find that nurses will seek opportunities with other employers to achieve their career goals.
3. Medical-surgical and telemetry units are challenging areas for new graduates because of higher patient ratios and growing patient acuity.
4. Many new graduates plan to return to graduate school to become NPs or CRNAs, and specialty experience is often required or highly desired in these programs.
5. The national turnover rate hovers around 18% as an average, but new graduate turnover in the first three years of practice is much higher.[20,22]

CONDUCT STAY INTERVIEWS

Retaining staff is challenging, so every new idea deserves consideration. According to the Society for Human Resource Management, the practice of STAY interviews is gaining momentum. Leaders conduct these interviews to understand why employees stay and what might cause them to leave. It also gives nurse leaders insight into what matters most to their staff. In an effective STAY interview, managers ask standard, structured questions casually and conversationally. The goal is to collect real-time information on what matters most to nurses and then individualize your retention strategies. Five questions to ask during this conversation are the following:[23]

Question 1: What do you look forward to each day when you commute to work?

This question brings nurses into the here and now and asks them to focus on their daily duties and challenges rather than expand on broader issues like pay and benefits. Employees stay and engage based on their relationships with supervisors and colleagues and how much they like what they do. These factors are often more important than pay and benefits.

Question 2: What are you learning here, and what do you want to learn?

This question helps leaders to direct their career coaching. Some nurses are ambitious to advance, some curious to learn more, and others just want to work and go home.

Question 3: Why do you stay here?

While appearing simple at first, this question opens doors for discovery about retention. Many staff have never thought about this, so the leader's role is to help them reflect. You might follow this first question with a second question about whether that was the only reason or whether they have other reasons.

Question 4: When is the last time you thought about leaving us, and what prompted it?

Everyone thinks about leaving a position at some point, so a directly worded question brings a much-needed conversation into the light.

Question 5: What can I do to make your job better for you?
While this question sends out a net for all remaining topics, it must ultimately yield answers about the interviewer. Avoiding defensiveness is critical. Be transparent about what you have influence over and areas that you may not.

Planning periodic STAY interviews is essential. In research on timing, Daniel Pink points out that many staff seriously consider leaving a position around their anniversary date with the organization.[24] They ask themselves – "*Do I still want to be here next year?*" Pink advises that nurse managers pay attention to anniversary dates and do STAY interviews 60-90 days before that date.

NURSING CARE DELIVERY MODELS

It is unlikely that we will see changes in the nursing workforce supply any time soon. Instead, we need to rethink the way we deliver nursing care. While primary nursing is still the most widely used delivery system, many health systems experimented with team nursing during COVID-19 to meet surge staffing requirements. Team nursing is based on a philosophy in which groups of professional and non-professional personnel work together to identify, plan, implement, and evaluate comprehensive client-centered care. The team is led by an experienced nurse team leader who delegates and oversees care provided to patients. Team members might include less experienced nurses, licensed practical nurses, and patient care technicians. A key concept is a group that works together toward a common goal, providing qualitative, comprehensive nursing care. Everyone should practice at the top of their scope of practice or job description.[25]

Another promising idea to address the nurse staffing issues on medical-surgical and telemetry unit is to convert them to EDUs or teaching units.[26] If the trend of short tenures of new graduates on these units is the new normal, why not make these units the educational units that most recent graduates transition through? The units could be staffed with seasoned educators or an attending nurse who works with the new graduates on all shifts. The staffing would need to reflect the change in skill mix. Depending on their long-term goals, recent graduates could be given *flight plans* to guide them through goals that need to be achieved before moving into specialty units. Moving forward into the future, nurse leaders will seek other innovative ways to meet their staffing and scheduling challenges through new nursing care delivery models.

KEY POINTS

✓ Staffing is one area where nurse leaders can both improve productivity and reduce costs.

✓ Many health systems use consensus panels to determine nursing care hours per patient day based on the specialty area's average acuity.

✓ The high replacement costs for an RN can quickly add up in large health systems, so unit turnover needs to be carefully tracked.

✓ A variance occurs when there is a difference between what is budgeted versus the expenses incurred.

✓ Nurse leaders who work in unionized environments have additional considerations to pay attention to when staffing or scheduling.

CHAPTER 19

DEVELOPING A STRATEGIC MINDSET

In today's rapidly changing healthcare environment, strategic thinking skills have become a critical differentiator among candidates for leadership advancement. Nurse leaders sometimes receive feedback that they are not strategic in their thinking. This feedback usually comes without any guidance on what to do about it. Developing a strategic mindset is a learnable skill, but it takes practice. It may feel uncomfortable at first. You should be willing to challenge the status quo and question assumptions when you frame strategic choices. To do this requires a clear understanding of strategically thinking through situations, developing strategic awareness, and linking strategic plans to frontline clinical work.

Strategic thinking is more than designing a plan of action. It is a way of thinking or mindset about the risk, profit, and cost of decisions or solutions.[27] In a now-classic article published in the January-February 2013 Harvard Business Review, Schoemaker, Krupp, and Howland identify six essential skills to become a more strategic thinker:[28]

1. **The ability to anticipate**

   Nurse leaders must be able to identify threats and opportunities to their units and organizations. You need to be able to read the signposts. Demography is an important indicator of changes in the environment. For example, if you are a labor and delivery manager, you will want to track the projected birthrates in your community to anticipate increases or decreases in volumes.

2. **A willingness to challenge assumptions**

   Strategic leaders are willing to challenge the status quo. They understand that although they may currently be providers of choice in some areas, this could radically change with a reimbursement shift. Strategic thinkers can look ahead at the potential impact of new technologies such as robotics and challenge assumptions about whether some traditional tasks need to be done by nurses.

3. **Recognize patterns and interpret the environment**

   Influential leaders can see patterns in the environment that could lead to change. Sometimes data can be ambiguous, and one needs to look at the bigger picture to assess implications. Strategic nurse leaders are currently examining the long-term impact of the COVID crisis on the nursing workforce.

4. **Make the tough decisions**

   Decision making in tough times is both an art and a science. As we discussed in Chapter 5, some leaders and organizations err on the side of not moving quickly enough. When leaders wait too long to initiate change, they can lose opportunities and possibly market share.

5. **Align all the stakeholders**

   Strategic leaders should seek common ground with their stakeholders and ready their environments for change in advance. Truth-telling to the staff about the realities of an organization is vital. Two of the most effective strategies are to communicate early and often about changes in the environment.

6. Look for lessons learned

The most effective leaders are continuous learners and look for lessons learned in every situation. The ability to honestly reflect on one's leadership decisions and actions is key to becoming a more strategic leader.

Honing your strategic thinking skills is essential to your leadership development. Max wanted to advance in his health system but was passed over twice for an assistant chief nursing officer position. There were concerns about his ability to think strategically and take more of a systems perspective. Max was an expert in trauma care but would supervise a broad range of clinical services in the new role. In his current role, he was perceived as a detail-oriented "doer." His interview responses indicated that he had not kept pace with trends impacting other departments. In the ACNO role, he was expected to understand the relationships and interdependencies between departments and their challenges.

Systems thinking is the process of understanding how things influence one another within a whole. In health care organizations, the leader can look beyond one's work unit or department and consider how different parts of the organization work together to achieve outcomes. It is also the recognition that small changes in one area can have unanticipated consequences in other parts of the system if not carefully considered. Nurse leaders often attempt quick fixes to problems without thinking through the longer-term implications or the impact on different parts of the organization. They lack strategic awareness.

STRATEGIC AWARENESS

Max's dilemma is not unusual. Many nurse leaders struggle with strategic awareness. Max was determined to develop these skills. He sought mentorship from a respected ACNO in his system. Developing a strategic approach in your thinking requires a different way of looking at your environment. Like many nurse leaders, Max had a "heads down" approach to his work and only focused on what was happening in his clinical area. To advance in leadership, he would need to become more aware of what was happening within and beyond his organization. His mentor suggested that he do the following to expand his strategic awareness:[29]

- Spend time with his mentor attending executive meetings and then debrief about meeting decisions and organizational strategic directions.
- Evaluate the changing conditions in his community, such as demographic trends and consumer expectations.
- Ask tough questions and be curious in discussions with patients, families, staff, and other stakeholders. Invite opposing viewpoints to challenge your thinking.
- Evaluate workforce trends, both locally and nationally, then assess the trend's potential impact moving forward.
- Track what is happening with the economy and political legislation because this can ultimately impact reimbursement and regulation.
- Expand his reading to understand what is happening in related industries such as pharmaceuticals, medical suppliers, and insurers.
- Monitor trends in technologies and consider, *"What, if anything, does this mean to us in our health system?"*
- Take time out to be more reflective in analyzing changing trends in his environment over time. Ask yourself: *"What's not working here anymore, and what do we need to do about it?"*

Strategic Plans

Organizations use strategic plans to guide decision making about resource use and future directions. With the turbulence in the healthcare environment, today's strategic plans have a much shorter timeframe, usually two to five years. The cornerstone of a strategic plan is the organization's mission, vision, and values statement. As an example, the Veterans Healthcare Systems (VHA) has the following mission, vision, and values statement:[30]

Mission - Honor America's veterans by providing exceptional health care that improves their health and well-being.

Vision - VHA will continue to be the benchmark of excellence and value in health care and benefits by providing exemplary services that are patient-centered and evidence-based. This care will be delivered by engaged, collaborative teams in an integrated environment that supports learning, discovery, and continuous improvement. It will emphasize prevention and population health and contribute to the nation's well-being through education, research, and service in national emergencies.

Values – Integrity, Commitment, Advocacy, Respect, and Excellence.

When strategic planning decisions occur, the mission, vision, and values statement should guide its planning and work. For example, education and research are part of the VHA vision. When VHA nurse leaders are involved in strategic planning, they need to consider academic and research partnerships. It is an organizational expectation and not just a nice to do. Nurse leaders should review the strategic plan of their organization. These plans provide valuable insight into the goals and priorities. Budget resources are usually linked to the strategic objectives of the organization. Expansion in one area can mean fewer resources for other services. Wise leaders try to connect any new budget requests to the organization's strategic plan.

THE SWOT ANALYSIS

A commonly used tool in strategic planning is a SWOT analysis. It helps identify the strengths, weaknesses, opportunities, and threats as you plan new initiatives or evaluate your competitive environment. The tool has value because it requires you to think through your strategic decisions by analyzing aspects of both the internal and external environment.[31]

Strengths are internal to the environment. You assess what you are doing well and what resources are available.

Weaknesses are internal to the environment. You assess what could be improved and what resources you are lacking.

Opportunities are external to the environment. What trends or partnerships could you use to your advantage?

Threats are external to the environment. What is your competition doing, and what could harm you in the future?

Bryce learned about the SWOT analysis in a leadership development program. Recruitment and retention of nurses were challenging in his critical-care unit. He wanted to be strategic in designing a plan. Bryce asked his unit practice council to do a SWOT analysis using recruitment and retention as their strategic challenge. The committee presented Bryce with their assessment (Figure 13). After reviewing the SWOT analysis, the team decided to focus their efforts on building a stronger partnership for senior student practicums with their local university. They would market their student loan repayment plan as an attractive recruitment incentive. They also would develop a proposal to redesign the critical care unit as a dedicated education unit (DEU).

FIGURE 13

SWOT Analysis – Critical Care Recruitment

Strengths (Internal to Unit)	Weaknesses (Internal to Unit)
Beacon Designated ICU	50% of New Graduates Leave in First 3 Years
Highly Engaged Staff	Limited Continuing Education Resources
Strong Critical Care Residency Program	No Self-Scheduling
90% of Staff are CCRN Certified	Union Contract Slows Hiring
Dedicated Critical Care Clinical Specialist	Open ICU Visitation Not Currently in Place
Student Loan Repayment Program	New Nurse Manager

Opportunities (External to Unit)	Threats (External to Unit)
Partnership with Local University	Another local Health System Raised Pay 20%
Strong Relationship with Local AACN Chapter	Other Agencies offer Scholarships to Nursing Students
Excellent Reputation for Care	Local Travel and Agency Contract Work for ICU Nurses
New Philanthropy Donor Interested in Critical Care	High Cost of Living Area
Staff Willing to Serve as Recruitment Ambassadors	

THINK LIKE A FUTURIST

An essential component of strategic thinking is strategic foresight or our ability to investigate the future. Thinking like a futurist has never been more critical. The mantra of the futurist is to learn, unlearn and then relearn. We need to be aware of the filters that we have when trying to evaluate change. Sometimes when we have a great deal of experience in an area, we can be the victim of educated incapacity because of our investment in what we already know. Our filtration systems can lead us to almost unconsciously discount what we see in our environment because they do not line up with our established perspectives.

Futurists warn that the trends that we see today are not necessarily the future but instead represent the present. They are already visible, not emerging, and represent only one aspect of strategic fore-sight. Cecily Sommers, an internationally known futurist, says that futuristic thinking means a willingness to look sideways, backward, forwards, and upside down to envision a perhaps unexpected future.[32] Environmental scanning is the lifeblood of strategic foresight. Futurists use the STEEP framework in their scanning—the social, technological, economic, environmental, and political drivers where trends are born. Social trends include factors such as demographic changes, communi-cation, and consumer behaviors. Technological trends may be the most apparent, but one must look beyond your industry when evaluating them. Economic trends include job availability, alternative payment systems, trade issues, entrepreneurship, and taxes. Environmental trends include climate change, built spaces, shifts to some geographic regions or cities, and ecosystem elements. Political trends can encompass ideas about individualism versus collectivism, individual rights, ideologies, and government regulations.

To see new trends and make the creative mind leaps to how they might impact health care, we need to retrain our brains in the following three ways: [33]

1. Change your perspective by choosing new experiences and meet-ing different people than you would ordinarily encounter. Frank Spencer of the Kedge Foresight group recommends that we immerse ourselves in different environments like ethnographers to explore human behavior and trends.[34]

2. Look under the hood and get curious about why things work the way that they do. Force yourself to consider a different side of an issue that you feel strongly about and listen to others' opinions. Read more broadly and pay attention to trends in social media.

3. Give it a rest, as some of our best thinking will come when our mind is less focused and can connect unrelated experiences in new ways. Futurists believe that to lead in today's super-accelerated

environment effectively; leaders need to be willing to test new ideas, imagine how things could be different, and create a better future.

To navigate the future, nurse leaders will need to expand their thinking, be willing to let go of sacred cows that may no longer be relevant and think like a futurist.

KEY POINTS

✓ Strategic thinking skills have become a critical differentiator among candidates for leadership advancement.

✓ Strategic decisions should be made with an understanding of the organization's competitive environment.

✓ Organizations use strategic plans to guide decision making about resource use and future directions.

✓ A commonly used tool in strategic planning is a SWOT analysis.

✓ An essential component of strategic thinking is strategic foresight or our ability to investigate the future.

CHAPTER 20

BUILDING YOUR INFLUENCE AND LEADERSHIP BRAND

O ur last chapter focuses on building your influence and leadership brand within your organization. These are usually not covered in leadership development programs yet influencing-building skills are critical in nursing leadership. John Maxwell reminds us that leadership is influence – nothing more and nothing less.[35] The most vital skill that we can have as professionals is our ability to influence others successfully. It can be a professional career game-changer when you become the person others look to for guidance and expert advice. Influencing skills come naturally to some, but most of us need to learn them over time. That is why developing behaviors that help to build influence are so important. Becoming influential takes time, dedication, and a strong sense of self.[36-37]

Some key behaviors that you need to develop to become more influential include the following:

- Remain vigilant in detecting and validating power plays and be willing to fight back.
- Be succinct and maintain composure in presenting your point of view in emotion-laden situations.
- Evaluate roles/committees/task forces in one's organization for the level of power and influence that they have.
- Learn to ask for help or what you want, even when it might be uncomfortable.
- Recognize that likeability is overrated and will not necessarily lead to influence in an organization.
- Build social capital through an efficient and effective network both inside and outside the organization.
- Act and speak with power and influence, even in situations where you may not be confident.
- Work on establishing a positive first impression in your interactions.
- Overcome your hesitancy to self-promote and establish a positive social media image.
- Manage your reputation carefully. Integrity is essential.
- Be resilient in overcoming opposition and setbacks.
- Recognize there is a cost to power and influence—you undergo more scrutiny.
- Never completely burn bridges that you may need to cross back over at another point in time.

Being an influential leader hinges on strong, mutually beneficial relationships rooted in clear communication, mentorship, empowerment, and shared accountability. It also involves a recognition that power plays and politics will always be part of organizational life. Resources are limited in organizations, and leaders must learn when to give in and when to go to battle.

Ariana learned this lesson when she accepted a quality director role in a large health system. She was recruited because the system had some compliance issues on their last Joint Commission survey. Ariana quickly identified some gaps in care and brought them to the attention of the medical director. He was not receptive to her suggested changes and immediately began to undermine her credibility by aggressively questioning her at committee meetings. Ariana recognized the behavior as a power play. This was one political battle that she realized she would have to fight to correct the deficits she identified successfully.

Choose Your Political Battles Wisely

Each of us in our leadership role has only a finite amount of time. While you may want to battle through every conflict because you feel you are "right," battles can take an enormous amount of time and personal energy. Choosing our battles wisely, as Ariana did, may make us much more effective in winning those that are important to us. Selecting those situations where the consequences matter to us will allow us to do a better job of preserving our energy, relationships, and peace of mind. To do this, we need to carefully assess each organizational situation and reflect on the following questions:

1. **Is this situation in my sphere of influence?**
   While something may bother you and be in your "circle of concern," as Dr. Covey described it (See Part 5), it may not be in our "circle of influence."[38] Ask whether you have real power to change the situation and whether there is a strong likelihood that you can reverse the problem with your involvement. If the answer is no, it would be better to pass on the battle.

2. **Do I want to invest the social capital that this battle might involve?**
   A wise mentor once told me that you could win the battle but lose the war because people do not forget. You do not need to fight

every battle just because you feel challenged. Carefully consider how pursuing a battle will be viewed within the organization and whether the outcomes will be worth the relationships that might get damaged through arguments. Just being right may not be enough to invest. Is this battle even worth your time? As a leader, you do not have an unlimited supply of social capital and goodwill in your organization, so it is vital to use it wisely.

3. Is this my battle to fight?

Some battles are none of our business, but others want to involve us. Think through carefully any show of support in a battle that you agree to provide to someone else. Personal relationships can easily pull us into situations where we take a side and invest energy only to regret it in the long run because there was no real "right" or "wrong" on the issue.

4. What is the long-term impact if I do nothing?

We should always leave "doing nothing" as an option to consider. If the conflict does not involve a serious professional, ethical, or legal issue, there may be no long-term impact if you do nothing. There may be no absolute right or wrong in the situation. It takes a stronger person to let things go rather than jumping into the fray and over-reacting. Thinking beyond the short term is an immensely powerful, albeit underutilized, leadership strategy.

Your leadership battles can either be dealt with now or left alone and accepted as part of the present moment, which could change. Ideally, as leaders, we would love a conflict-free organization where battles never happen, but this is unrealistic. In these situations, the most powerful weapon we have is control over our own behavior. Carefully choosing your battles may ultimately prove to be much wiser than fighting through every organizational disagreement.

INFLUENCING SKILLS

The ability to successfully influence others is the essence of leadership. Whether attempting to change someone's mindset or seeking support for a new initiative, you use influencing skills. One of the most powerful books ever written on influencing is Dale Carnegie's, *How to Win Friends and Influence People*.[39] Carnegie was the first to recognize that influencing is an art that begins with trying to put yourself in the other person's shoes. Ten of his most classic ideas on how to do this include the following:

- "If you want to gather honey, don't kick over the beehive – criticism is a dangerous spark."
- "Show people how what you are proposing helps them to achieve their goals – appeal to nobler motives."
- "Develop a genuine interest in others and their work before you ask them to do something."
- "Learn to smile often."
- "Use people's names in your conversation."
- "Make the other person feel important."
- "Show respect and sympathy for the opinions and ideas of others – even if you disagree."
- "When you are wrong – admit it quickly and emphatically."
- "Begin difficult conversations in a friendly way – starting with areas that you can agree on."
- "Do less talking and more listening."

Through his work in sales, Carnegie developed a keen sense of what drives human behavior. He understood how vital reciprocity is to building influence. A more contemporary approach called the SCARF model was developed by David Rock.[40] Rock suggests that your ability to influence behavior depends on minimizing the risks and maximizing the other person's rewards. Our brain views new ideas or initiatives as threats. We use the following filters to determine whether we will allow ourselves to be influenced:

Status – Are you respectful of my status, or is what you are asking me to do going to change my status in the eyes of others?

Certainty – Can I predict what will happen here, or are there risks in this situation for me?

Autonomy – Do I have control over what is happening, or are you asking me to give up some of my rights?

Relatedness – Can I relate to you? Are you like me? Am I comfortable with you?

Fairness – Is what you are asking for fair? Are you taking something from me?

Kyle saw the power in using the SCARF model as he made the argument for moving his health system from one electronic health record to another. The biggest challenge to the change came from the medical staff. Kyle realized that some of the older physicians were not comfortable with technology. They worried about their status, the risks, and threats with the change. Kyle spent a great deal of time presenting the new record's ease and how it would save them time in their charting. He also emphasized the clinical record customization he could provide to them with the new EHR and the smoother interface with their home computers.

BUILD A STRONG LEADERSHIP BRAND

A strategic way to build influence in an organization is to think of yourself as a brand. Jeff Bezos, the founder of Amazon, once commented that your brand is what people say about you when you are not in the room. You may not think you have one, but the reality is that you do. Your leadership brand is what you are known for and how you present yourself to the world. It is the impression that you make and the reputation that you have. It is how you present yourself to the world and what your impact is. Done correctly, you can use it to enhance your influence and leverage career success. There are three ways that you can build a strong leadership brand:

1. BE AUTHENTIC

Your brand must be true to who you are as a person because ultimately, others will define your brand for you through the actions they see you take. Your brand should be consistent with your core values that we discussed in Chapter 3. Consistency is essential to your brand. Do what you say you will do. If your behaviors do not support the image you want to create, you will not successfully build the brand that you want to have.

2. BE KNOWN FOR SOMETHING

You must know yourself and your strengths. All of us have some things that we do better than most people – what are those for you? If you were a product with a tagline – what would that be for you? Take the time to speak with many different colleagues to understand your strengths and then use it to create your brand. Ask yourself how you make people feel or what benefits people receive from working with you. Knowing about yourself and how you can best do this is essential to being successful. If you have a LinkedIn page and others have endorsed, you – what have they endorsed you for? In your leadership toolkit (Part 5), there is a brand worksheet that includes questions you can ask.

3. WATCH YOUR ONLINE PRESENCE

Today, the first-place others may look to learn more about you is online. What does your online presence say about you? Do you regularly Google yourself to see what information about you is prominent? Are your online pictures professional and do they convey the type of image you want to send? Are you using LinkedIn to manage your professional identity and connect with others? If you are not, you are missing an opportunity to build your brand.

Once you have created a brand for yourself – be sure to be consistent with that brand and use it to help guide your decision-making and how you spend your time and energy. All of us want to believe that as leaders, we will have an impact. But this is not a given, and to have impact and influence, we must be intentional in our leadership. In their book *Be a Person of Impact,* authors Jackie and Kevin Freiberg suggest that leaders should ask themselves the following questions:[41]

1. When you attend a meeting or have a phone call scheduled on an important topic, are you better prepared than anyone else?
2. Do people applaud your sense of urgency and responsiveness to requests?
3. Do you take creativity and execution to the next level?
4. Do you know your organization's strategic direction so you can position yourself and staff to respond to the changes?
5. Are you willing to tackle challenges or take on initiatives that no one else wants?
6. When you talk to patients, do you try to learn as much as you can about them to understand your market better?
7. Do you have a reputation for doing your homework when you make presentations or bring forward requests?
8. Do you go above and beyond?
9. Do you hold yourself accountable for what you agree to do?
10. Do you ask for feedback to assess how others perceive you?

Impactful leaders understand the need to stretch their minds through reading and discussions with others. They focus on being connoisseurs in their areas of expertise and understand that "busyness" in and of itself does not make one productive. An impactful leader dares to try and is open to the new ideas brought forth by staff. Thinking one has the answers all the time or being right is highly overrated.

Exit with a Strong Leadership Brand

Throughout this book, we have talked about leading within an organization. At some point in your career, you may decide it is time to leave an organization. How you do this can either help or hurt your leadership brand. Quitting can be challenging because it does involve many losses. We spend almost as much time at work as we do at home. Nurse leaders are usually very invested in their work and their team even when things are not going well. Carla faced this dilemma. She had been with her health system for fifteen years, but the culture had changed, and so had she. Still, it was hard to leave a place where she had worked for most of her career. She sought some coaching to help her with the decision.

Carla's coach asked her to write down the pros and cons of her current position. Doing this is helpful as a first step in assessment. There are times when the cons may far outweigh the pros, making the decision easier. She also suggested that Carla reflect on the following questions:

1. **Have I become negative or unhappy about my job?** – It is vital to assess your personal feeling about your job. Have your professional concerns spilled over into your personal life? Your job may be negatively impacting both your health and relationships with friends and family.

2. **Am I still passionate about the work that I am doing?** – You will want to consider whether you are still passionate about

your work. In asking yourself this question, you may find that you are no longer passionate about the work and have begun to feel burned out. As we age, it also makes sense to consider our energy level and whether we can sustain the pace in our role.

3. **Is this organization still a good cultural fit for me?** – Whether we like it or not, an organization's culture evolves in response to leadership changes and environmental pressures. You may no longer feel congruence between your values and the leadership you work with.

4. **Are my ideas being heard, or have I lost influence?** – Chemistry is essential on teams. When leadership changes, you may discover that your opinions are not as valued as they once were. The first sign that it is time to leave for some leaders is when they find that they no longer invited to critical decision-making meetings.

5. **Is my pay today commensurate with my responsibilities?** – No one wants to feel undervalued for their work. In organizations today, leaders often find themselves taking on additional responsibilities with no increase in salary. They may also learn that their organization is paying a higher salary to newer team members with less experience.

6. **Are my skills being utilized to the fullest?** – Self-development is important to work satisfaction. All of us want to continue to grow in our work through stretch assignments and unique development opportunities. If this is not happening, you may feel your career has stalled.

The decision to leave a position can take courage. Most leaders err on the side of waiting too long. If you do decide to leave, planning is critical. It is always easier to seek a position (unless retirement is the next step) while you are still employed. Sometimes the decision is not yours, and you are asked to resign. The following are tips if that happens to you:

1. **Don't stay too long because your position power will begin to decline immediately**
Although your inclination may be to stay for thirty days to help get things for a transition, this may not be the best plan in this situation. Stay long enough to tie up loose ends but recognize that you are no longer part of the organization. You may not be included in decision making by other members of the executive team.

2. **Don't keep rehashing the situation in your mind**
There are many reasons why working relationships do not work out, often having little to do with job performance. Sometimes it is a financial decision to restructure or a new leader's desire to bring in a candidate they have worked with in other organizations.

3. **Remain positive with your team**
You are leaving your position, but your team will continue in your absence. They need time to grieve your loss as a leader and will look to you for guidance. Do not play the role of victim. Stay upbeat. Minimize any negative remarks that you make about the organization.

4. **Demonstrate class in all your actions but seek an assurance that you will receive a favorable recommendation and a severance package if available**
It is essential to set yourself up for a good recommendation, especially when you have been with an employer for ten years. Check out any benefits that you are entitled to as you leave, including a severance package.

5. **Give yourself time to think about your next professional move**
Although it may be tempting to jump right back into a job search, it is crucial to consider your next career step seriously. In some ways,

losing a job can be very liberating because it opens a wide range of possibilities in terms of what you would like to do next.

6. Reconnect with your network

If you have been with one employer for ten years, there is a strong chance that your current professional network outside your work environment might be weak. This is a time to reconnect with colleagues and join LinkedIn if you are not in that social network. Most great jobs come from colleague referrals so let everyone know that you are looking.

When one door closes, another one opens. It may take time, but it does happen. Keep in mind that ultimately, you are the architect of your transition, so make sure that you can feel proud about your behavior during this difficult time. Doing so will preserve your leadership brand.

View Leadership as a Journey

Whether you are in your first leadership role or are a seasoned leader, it is helpful to view your leadership career as a journey rather than a destination. Taking a leadership role is only the first step. Leaders have their ups and downs. Be sure to celebrate your successes but remember that there is always something new to learn. In Chapter 7, we talked about promoting a growth versus a fixed mindset when coaching staff. As a leader, you too need to have a growth mindset about your work.

When you have a growth mindset, you believe that you can and will develop a strong leadership brand over time. Even when you fail — and you are human, so you will fail from time to time — you will not be defeated. Instead of giving up and leaving leadership, you will begin to look at every situation as a learning experience. When you fail, you will figure out what went wrong and make sure it does not happen next time. You will not write yourself off and will step outside your comfort zone. When you adopt a growth mindset, you look for opportunities to improve yourself, often through ongoing education. Even if you are a recognized expert in a specific subject, it is always possible to learn new things. Leaders with a growth mindset seek out mentorship and ask a lot of questions. They recognize that they can learn from the struggles and experiences of others. To cultivate a growth mindset, acknowledge that you are a work in progress. You have accepted a challenge and are on an exciting journey to become the best leader that you can be.

KEY POINTS

✓ The most critical capacity that we have as professionals is our ability to influence others successfully.

✓ Your ability to influence behavior depends on minimizing the risks and maximizing the other person's rewards.

✓ At some point in your career, you may decide to resign from an organization – be sure to exit with your leadership brand intact.

✓ When you have a growth mindset, you believe that you can and will develop a strong leadership brand over time.

PART 4 REFERENCES

1. Hankin A. (January 2020 Investopedia). How US Healthcare Costs Compare to Other Countries. Available at https://www.investopedia.com/articles/personal-finance/072116/us-healthcare-costs-compared-other-countries.asp

2. Begley R, Cipriano P, Nelson T. The Business of Caring: Promoting Optimal Allocation of Nursing Resources. 2020. Available at https://www.hfma.org/content/dam/hfma/Documents/industry-initiatives/business-of-caring-promoting-optimal-allocation-nursing-resources.pdf

3. Penner SJ. *Economics and Financial Management for Nurses and Nurse Leaders.* New York: Springer; 2017.

4. Definitive HC. 2020 Trend Report. Definitive Healthcare Breaking Down US Hospital Payor Mix. Available at https://www.definitivehc.com/resources/healthcare-insights/breaking-down-us-hospital-payor-mixes

5. AHA 2020. Bundled Payment. https://www.aha.org/bundled-payment

6. CMS 2020. The Hospital Value Based Purchasing Program. Available at https://www.cms.gov/Medicare/Quality-Initiative

s-Patient-Assessment-Instruments/Value-Based-Programs/HVBP/
Hospital-Value-Based-Purchasing

7. CMS 2020. The Hospital Readmission Reduction Program. Available at https://www.cms.gov/Medicare/Quality-Initiative s-Patient-Assessment-Instruments/Value-Based-Programs/HRRP/ Hospital-Readmission-Reduction-Program

8. CMS 2020. The Hospital-Acquired Condition Reduction Program Available at https://www.cms.gov/Medicare/ Medicare-Fee-for-Service-Payment/AcuteInpatientPPS/ HAC-Reduction-Program

9. The Affordable Care Act 2020 Available at Affordable Care Act (ACA) Definition (investopedia.com)

10. CMS 2020. The Emergency Medical Treatment and Labor Act. Available at https://www.cms.gov/Regulations-and-Guidance/ Legislation/EMTALA

11. American Action Forum (April 22nd, 2020) The Future of America's Entitlements: What You Need to Know About the Medicare and Social Security Trustees Reports. Available at https://www.americanactionforum.org/research/the-future-of-america s-entitlements-what-you-need-to-know-about-the-medicare-and-soci al-security-trustees-reports-3/

12. Baxter C, Warshawsky N. Exploring the acquisition of nurse manager competence. Nurse Leader. 12(1) 46-51, 59; 2014.

13. Cleveland Clinic QD Consult. Cutting the cost of supplies. Available at https://consultqd.clevelandclinic.org/cutting-the-cost-of-supplies/

14. Johnston L. Reducing Patient Supply Waste through Nursing Education to Improve Quality of Care in the Clinical Microsystem. (2017) Available at Reducing Patient Supply Waste Through Nurse Education to Improve Quality of Patient Care in the Clinical Microsystem (usfca.edu)

15. Aiken LH, Cimiotti, JP, Sloane, DM, Smith HL., Flynn L, Neff DF. (Effects of nurse staffing and education on patient deaths in

hospitals with different work environments. *Medical Care. 49(10),* 1047-1053; 2011

16. AHRQ PSNet. 2019 Nurse Staffing and Patient Safety. Available at https://psnet.ahrq.gov/primer/nursing-and-patient-safety

17. Handoff Podcast Interview with Therese Fitzpatrick (September 2020) Available at

18. https://www.trustedhealth.com/the-handoff-podcast/therese-fitzpatrick

19. ANA Principles for Nurse Staffing 2019 3rd Edition Available at https://www.nursingworld.org/practice-policy/nurse-staffing/

20. Registered Nurse.Org (June 20th, 2020) Do Unions Benefit or Harm Nursing and Healthcare Industries. Available at https://www.registerednursing.org/do-unions-benefit-harm-healthcare-nursing/

21. NSI Nursing Solutions (2020). National Healthcare Retention & RN Staffing Report. Available at https://www.nsinursingsolutions.com/Documents/Library/NSI_National_Health_Care_Retention_Report.pdf

22. Virkstis K., Herleth A, Rewers L. Closing nursing's experience-complexity gap. *Journal of Nursing Administration.* 49(12). 580-582; 2019.

23. Press Ganey Nursing Special Report 2018. Optimizing the Nursing Workforce: Key Drivers of Intent to Stay for Newly Licensed and Experienced Nurses. Available at 2018 Nursing Special Report (pressganey.com)

24. Finnegan R. (SHRM Website August 14th, 2018).Conducting Stay Interviews. Available at https://www.shrm.org/resourcesandtools/hr-topics/employee-relations/pages/how-to-conduct-stay-interviews-part-2.aspx

25. Pink DH. *When: The Scientific Secrets of Perfect Timing.* New York: Riverhead Books; 2018.

26. Sherman RO. (November 23rd, 2020 Emerging RN Leader Blog). Team Nursing Revisited – Again. Available at Team Nursing Revisited - Again - Emerging Nurse Leader (emergingrnleader.com)

27. Dedicated Education Units. Available at Dedicated Education Units | School of Nursing (uconn.edu)

28. Tajpour, Mehdi, et al. "The Effect of Managers Strategic Thinking on Opportunity Exploitation." *Scholedge International Journal of Multidisciplinary & Allied Studies ISSN 2394-336X*, vol. 5, no. 6, 2018, p. 68.

29. Schoemaker PJH, Krupp S, Howland S. Strategic leadership: Essential Skills. *Harvard Business Review*. January-February 2013, p. 131-134.

30. Sherman RO, Cohn T. How to develop a strategic mindset: Follow these steps to think more strategically. *American Nurse Today*. 14(5) 14-16; 2019.

31. Department of Veterans Affairs. Mission, Vision, Values. Available at https://www.va.gov/about_va/mission.asp

32. Mindtools. 2020 SWOT Analysis: How to develop a strategy for success. Available at https://www.mindtools.com/pages/article/newTMC_05.htm

33. Sommers C. Think Like a futurist: Know What Changes, What Doesn't and What's Next. San Francisco, CA: Jossey-Bass; 2013.

34. Sherman RO. Thinking like a futurist. *Nurse Leader. 15*(1), 12-13; 2017.

35. Spencer F. (2016) Strategic Foresight Primer. Published by the Kedge Group.

36. Maxwell J. *The 21 irrefutable laws of leadership*. Nashville: Thomas Nelson; 2007.

37. Pfeffer J. *Power: Why Some People Have It and Others Don't*. New York: Harper Collins; 2010.

38. Patterson K, Grenny J, Maxfield D, Switzler A. *Influencer*. New York: McGraw-Hill; 2008.

39. Covey S. The 7 habits of highly effective people: Powerful lessons in personal change. New York: Fireside Books; 1989.

40. Carnegie D. *How to win friends and influence people*. New York: Simon and Shuster; 1935.

41. Rock, D. (2013). The SCARF Model Influencing others. Available at https://www.youtube.com/watch?v=rh5Egsa-bg4
42. Freiberg K, Freiberg J. *Be a Person of Impact: 12 Strategies to be CEO of Your Life*. Create Space Publishing; 2015.

PART 5

YOUR LEADERSHIP TOOLKIT

*"Leadership and learning are
indispensable to one another."*

JOHN F. KENNEDY

A 100 Day Nurse Leader Action Plan

Competency Area	Action Steps
Personal Mastery	1. Meet 1:1 with your boss to clarify his/her expectations. 2. Request a leader-mentor in the organization. 3. Review your position description & evaluation criteria. 4. Determine what committees/meetings you should attend. 5. Avoid making any significant changes.
Interpersonal Effectiveness	1. Meet 1:1 with each direct report and ask what is going well on the unit, what needs to change, their unique strengths, and what they expect of you. 2. Schedule meetings with key stakeholders such as pharmacy, central supply, ED, nutrition, quality improvement. 3. Hold your first staff meeting. 4. Inform staff of your communication style (see the staff guide to working with you).
Human Resource Management	1. Review the position descriptions of each staff position and evaluation criteria. 2. Learn about the HR recruitment process to fill vacancies. 3. Review unit/department turnover data. 4. Determine the HR process for managing performance issues and challenges. 5. Read the union contract if applicable. 6. Evaluate the staffing/scheduling process used in your area. 7. Compile a staff profile – generation/years of experience/time on unit/certifications.

Competency Area	Action Steps
Financial Management	1. Clarify your role in the budget process and the budget cycle. 2. Review every cost center in your budget and get help if needed from the CFO. 3. Assess the use of overtime/sick leave/FMLA on the unit. 4. Determine how equipment is requested and price threshold for a capital equipment request.
Systems Thinking	1. Review six months of performance data and the top 5 DRGs for the unit/department. 2. Focus on solving at least one frustrating process or problem for staff in your area to achieve an early win. 3. Assess the political and cultural issues in the organization. 4. Review the strategic plan/payer mix for the organization. 5. Review the organizational chart.
Caring for Self/ Staff/Patients	1. Set your work hours to maintain your equilibrium and a sustainable pace. 2. Choose at least one resiliency behavior to implement into your daily schedule. 3. Establish a routine for leader/patient rounding. 4. Develop a process to recognize staff regularly.

© Rose O Sherman, 2021

A Staff Guide to
Working with You

Introduction – Provide a little background information about yourself and why you are writing the guide. What are your goals for the manual?

How do you view success – What are the values that underpin your understanding of success. What is your leadership philosophy that drives your management style?

How you communicate – What is your communication style? What are your preferred methods of communication (in person, email, text, phone)? How do you like to conduct staff meetings, and what are your expectations around staff participation? Are there any aspects of communication that you are weak in but working on (e.g. abrupt in conversations, straightforward communicator)?

Things about me that may annoy others – What are some of the things about your leadership style that your staff may misunderstand. What are the quirks that could unintentionally annoy a different personality type? Are you introverted? Do you dislike small talk? Do you like to know about your staff member's families?

What gains or loses your trust – What qualities do you value that help build trust? What triggers cause you to lose faith (e.g. gossiping, failing to keep commitments)?

What are your strengths – What do you love to do and help others with (e.g. coach staff, teach, de-escalate crises)?

What are blind spots or areas you are working on – If you are working on weaknesses that staff can help you with – let them know (e.g. develop more tact, be more timely with feedback, set reminders about following up on unit problems).

What are your expectations of staff – What do you consider professional behavior? Do you have expectations of your team that might be different than other managers? What is excellent customer service from your perspective?

What is your philosophy about giving and receiving feedback – How do you provide coaching and feedback (just in time or on a more scheduled basis)? How should staff provide you with feedback if there are problems with the unit? What are your expectations around teamwork and conflict resolution?

Designed using ideas from Julie Zho https://lg.substack.com/p/the-looking-glass-a-user-guide-to

GO-TO QUESTIONS FOR
DIFFICULT CONVERSATIONS

What do you know for sure about this situation?

Is there another explanation for what you observed here?

What could you have done differently in this situation?

What impact could a failure to improve have on your professional success?

How do you know for sure that what you are telling me is true?

What role have you played in this situation?

What are you going to do to help resolve this issue?

Tell me what great would look like right now?

What would be the most helpful thing that you could do in this situation?

Would you rather be right or happy?

How can we make this work?

What would happen if you chose to agree and help?

What is missing in this situation? How could you change that?

What if both points of view are right?

How might you be wrong in your perceptions?

How is thinking like this keeping you stuck?

How can we improve morale?

Can I count on you to show up differently?

How can you turn a negative opinion into a positive action here?

What would add more value here – your opinion or positive action?

What story are you telling yourself about what is happening here?

How do you think others perceive your attitude?

RESILIENCY GROW MODEL COACHING TEMPLATE

Name: _____ Date: _____

GROW Model Step	Questions to Ask	Coach Notes Column
Goal Type **Clarification** **Personal well-being and resiliency in a time of change**	What is on your mind? What is the real challenge here for you in this situation? What are you most worried about? What would you like to have happen that is not happening now? How will we know if we have met your goal expectations?	
Reality **Clarify the current situation** **Check assumptions** **Identify obstacles** **(time, money, environment, people, self-beliefs)**	Tell me more about what is happening now? How do you know your perceptions about this situation are accurate? What impact or effect is your stress having on your well-being? What needs to be true that is not true today for you to be less anxious and more resilient? What personal changes will you need to make?	
Options **Brainstorm choices** **Select** **preferred options**	What approaches could you use? What have you done in similar situations when you have felt stressed? What could we do in the work setting to help reduce your anxiety? What is your preferred option? What will happen if you do nothing?	
Way Forward **Develop an action plan with time** **Sensitive actions and clear Outcomes**	What is your first step? What is your timeframe? What could get in the way? What support do you need from me? What follow-up should we plan?	

Coaching Guide Nurse Leader Coach ® 2021

The Circle of Influence Tool

Knowing What We Can and Can't Control

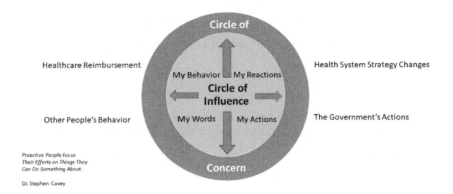

Healthcare Reimbursement

Health System Strategy Changes

Other People's Behavior

The Government's Actions

Proactive People Focus Their Efforts on Things They Can Do Something About.

Dr. Stephen Covey

Questions to Ask Staff

1. Is this issue we are discussing in your circle of influence or your circle of concern?
2. What can you do in your circle of influence to impact this situation?
3. How could implementing that behavior expand your circle of influence in this situation?
4. What actions should you be taking in this situation but are not yet doing?
5. What would be the consequences here if you fail to change this behavior?

Adapted from Covey SR. *The 7 Habits of Highly Effective People.* Simon & Schuster; 1989.

To Build Your Brand - Know Who You Are as Leader

People with strong brands are clear about who they are, their purpose, and how they can add value in situations. Answer the following questions about who you are.

1. What are the major strengths that others see in me and that I want to be known for?

2. When working on teams, how do I add value?

3. When I face obstacles, what are my "go-to skills" to overcome them?

4. My expert knowledge is in the following areas:

5. The most successful project I ever tackled was:

6. I want to be known for my expert work in this area:

7. The customer, target audience, or "tribe" for my work is:

Read and Listen to Lead
– Free Resources

Coaching for Leaders Podcast This is an excellent weekly podcast by Dave Stachowiak designed to provide you with practice wisdom about leadership. Dave (a former Dale Carnegie executive leader) runs a global leadership academy and has interviewed leading experts on the podcast since 2011. You can subscribe for free at Coaching for Leaders - Leadership podcast by Dave Stachowiak

Emerging RN Leader Website Author: Dr. Rose O Sherman posts twice-weekly blogs (Monday and Thursday) on leadership topics targeted to developing healthcare and nursing leaders. Many blogs include free leadership resources. www.emergingrnleader.com

Fierce Healthcare Fierce Healthcare is a daily newsletter that is a leading source of healthcare management news. This is an excellent resource for nurse leaders on a wide range of healthcare leadership topics. Subscriptions are free. http://www.fiercehealthcare.com/

Health Leaders Media Health Leaders Media evaluates all current healthcare information and sends a weekly summary of what is essential for nurse leaders to know. Subscribe for free at HealthLeaders: Get Critical Updates to Move Your Organization Forward (healthleadersmedia.com)

Kaiser Health News Kaiser Health News (KHN) is a nonprofit news organization committed to in-depth coverage of health care policy and politics of interest to healthcare leaders. A free email news subscription is available. http://kaiserhealthnews.org/

Read to Lead Podcast This is a weekly leadership podcast built on the philosophy that the best leaders are readers. Jeff Brown interviews authors of the newest leadership books and discusses key learnings from the books. https://readtoleadpodcast.com/

SmartBrief on Leadership SmartBrief on Leadership provides various articles and blog postings related to innovative leadership and management ideas. Users can subscribe, and updates are sent directly through email. https://www2.smartbrief.com/signupSystem/subscribe. action?pageSequence=1&briefName=leadership&utm_source=brief

TED Talks on Leadership TED is a nonprofit devoted to ideas worth spreading. It started (in 1984) as a conference bringing together people from three worlds: **Technology, Entertainment, Design.** The TED talks on leadership are excellent short videos from some of the most creative thinkers in the world on leadership. http://www.ted.com/ search?cat=ss_all&q=leadership

About the Author

Rose O. Sherman, EdD, RN, NEA-BC, FAAN, is nationally known for her work in helping current and future nurse leaders to develop their leadership skills. Rose is an emeritus professor at the Christine E. Lynn College of Nursing at Florida Atlantic University and currently serves as a faculty member in the Marian K Shaughnessy Nursing Leadership Academy at Case Western Reserve University. She received a BA in political science and BSN in nursing from the University of Florida. Her master's degree in nursing is from the Catholic University of American, and she has a doctorate in nursing leadership from Columbia University in New York City. Before teaching, she spent twenty-five years in leadership roles with the Department of Veterans Affairs at five VA Medical Centers.

Rose is the editor of *Nurse Leader,* the American Organization of Nurse Executives' official journal. She writes a popular leadership blog www.emergingrnleader.com that is read by thousands of nurse leaders each week. Rose is a fellow in the American Academy of Nursing and an alumnus of the Robert Wood Johnson Executive Nurse Fellowship program. She is a Gallup-certified strengths coach and author of the book,

The Nurse Leader Coach: Become the Boss No One Wants to Leave. In 2020, Rose received the Pioneering Spirit Award by the American Association of Critical-Care nurses for her innovative work in developing nurse leaders. Contact Rose at roseosherman@outlook.com.

Bring the Nuts and Bolts of Nursing Leadership Program to Your Organization

Nurses are often promoted into leadership roles with little or no understanding of the leadership and business skills needed to succeed in the role. They pick up pieces of the leadership skillset but rarely have all the tools they need to transition into leadership. From leadership and communication to the business knowledge necessary to run a unit or department effectively, let us design a customized, affordable one or two-day leadership program either live or virtual to provide your team with the essential skills they need. Before developing the program, we will assess your needs to plan content tailored to your organization. The program costs include this book, a program workbook, and a toolkit with your leaders' actionable resources. Our goal is to give your leaders the confidence they need to be successful in their role. You can learn more by contacting Rose O. Sherman at roseosherman@outlook.com

Made in the USA
Middletown, DE
17 July 2021